piano PROFESSIONAL s

The
Foundations
of Technique

Murray McLachlan

Produced and distributed by

FABER ff MUSIC

PUBLISHING SERVICES

© 2014 by Murray McLachlan
All rights administered worldwide by Faber Music Ltd
This edition first published in 2014
Bloomsbury House 74–77 Great Russell Street London WC1B 3DA
Music setting by Spartan Press Music Publishers Ltd.
Cover and text designed by Susan Clarke
Illustrations by Nancy Litten
Printed in England by Caligraving Ltd

ISBN10: 0-571-53275-6
EAN13: 978-0-571-53275-9

Contents

To Julian and Kathryn

Introduction

What exactly is piano technique? Is its cultivation really necessary? Is technique exclusively concerned with mechanical control? Does technical training mean years of drudgery and patience? Can anyone obtain technical control provided they spend enough time practising? Does technique lead an independent existence from musicality and artistry and therefore function as an unpleasant if essential necessity?

Too many students still believe that piano technique is somehow divorced from artistic creativity. The subject is unfairly stereotyped as something exclusively sporty and mechanical. It is assumed that speed, strength and accuracy are all that technique is about. Nothing could be further from the truth. All of the questions above can be swiftly answered in a couple of sentences herewith. Piano technique is about putting into practice everything that you wish to do. It is about fulfilling ambitions, hopes and desires. Technique makes dreams come true. It stands as a proverbial fairy figure from one of the Brothers Grimm tales: when technique is convincingly set up it seems to tell us 'Your wish is my command'.

Clearly you need to know what your heart desires before calling on your technique for assistance, but once your objectives are clear, then their successful realisation at the piano depends entirely on how effective your 'technique' fairy godmother is.

What follows is an adjusted and expanded version of some of the early articles written for *International Piano* magazine (www.internationalpiano.com) as a column entitled 'Masterclass' from 2001 to the present. This first book focuses on the essential foundations of piano playing. Beginning with considerations that enable a healthy posture and approach to develop at the instrument, it expands into a sequenced course of pianism that covers all the basic principles that are essential if a reliable technique is to be achieved.

The information presented is for everyone interested in piano playing. Because of this, it should be especially useful for teachers. The main information in each chapter is as relevant for beginners and intermediate players as for postgraduate students and professional concert pianists. It takes the spirit and approach of EPTA (the European Piano Teachers' Association, www.epta-uk.org) to heart in that it makes room for everyone who is interested in piano playing and teaching, at all levels. In this respect the approach may be rather different from that taken in other books on technique. We have technical exercises here that can easily be tackled by pre-grade 1 players. What is interesting is that these have proved to be just as helpful to the most advanced pianists as to beginners. Similarly examples from the most challenging works in the repertoire are included. Because it is so easy to listen to all of the repertoire in the 21st century on the internet, inexperienced players can follow these extracts via performances on YouTube, Spotify and so on. I believe that inspiration and enlightenment from the great masterpieces can help players at all levels. It seems wrong to exclude beginner pianists from opportunities for technical enlightenment from the most exciting music available. So no apology is included for saturating the text that follows with adventurous music, though of course young children may need to engage the attention of their parents at first in order to progress through the book, and beginner students of all ages would be well advised to work at the exercises and explanations in close association with their teachers.

As mentioned, this first instalment of some twenty chapters deals with foundations and much of what is considered standard technique. Part two will be concerned with putting technique into practice and acquiring the skills/tools/facility/capability (i.e. the 'technique') to play faster, stronger, more beautifully and with greater stamina. Memorising, practising, fingering, phrasing and voicing amongst other topics will be considered here. Finally, Part three will consider technique from a psychological basis. The technique of 'music in the mind' will mainly deal with how to control anxiety, remain focused, motivated, inspired, grow creatively and develop artistically. It will show how to consistently develop and expand techniques so that musical dreams and ambitions can truly become realities.

This book would not have been written without the unprompted commission from Julian Haylock back in 2000 to write articles on technique for *International Piano Quarterly*, as the magazine was then called. I remain indebted to the support of *International Piano* and to Rhinegold Publishing, especially to the help and encouragement from editors over the years, including Chloe Cutts and, currently, Claire Jackson. This book is the first in the 'Piano Professional series' – a really exciting new collaboration between Faber Music and EPTA UK. *Piano Professional* is the flagship magazine of EPTA UK and it is hoped that EPTA's values of supporting and encouraging piano teachers and their students will be given a new dimension via an ever-expanding and diversely exciting series of books related to the piano and teaching.

Murray McLachlan

1 Prevention is better than cure

'Technical security at the piano can only exist when the performer has achieved complete firmness in the fingertips along with total freedom and relaxation in the wrists, elbows and shoulders.'

In our increasingly injury-prone era it is vital that you have a firm understanding of what is good for your pianistic development and what is disastrous, before you even think of opening Hanon's celebrated 'The Virtuoso Pianist In Sixty Exercises'[1]. Too many students have ended up in hospital after plunging into a severe diet of five-finger exercises, executed *fortissimo* with raised digits for several hours a day, with no consideration being given to warming-up, hand position, posture and so on. In fact it is vital to start looking at your complete lifestyle if you want to remain in good physical shape at the instrument. That means diet, sleep patterns, exercise (physical and mental), relaxation techniques and posture. If you slouch or play with your neck jutting out, seek a good Alexander Technique teacher before doing anything else!

I would also argue that patience, lateral thinking, intellectual curiosity and even the ability to find humour in one's own sad pianistic lot are also indispensable for building up mechanical competence at the piano. If you are serious about improving your technique you do need to be dedicated, but not obsessively chained to the peculiarly sporty attractions of repetitive digital movements without input from your grey cells. I strongly believe that it is unacceptable for students to practise their scales or Pischna[2] studies whilst reading or watching television. By going into 'brain-dead' mode at the keyboard and getting a multi-packed thrill from all that adrenaline pumping through your system, you run the risk of inflicting lasting damage to your tendons. This can lead to being unable even to open a door for several months (as tragically I've seen), let alone get anywhere near a piano.

So, you've sorted-out your lifestyle, realised that technique is about intellect as much as coordination and physical development and you've found an Alexander teacher[3]. The next stage is to invest in an adjustable stool for all those hours of work in progress. Opinions vary as to how high you should sit, but if your back is not straight then you are too high, and if your shoulders are raised even slightly then you are too low. Pianists can learn a lot from t'ai chi regarding posture. Feet should be firmly anchored, at a slightly splayed angle,

---

1 Hanon 'The Virtuoso Pianist In Sixty Exercises' (1873) complete, Charles-Louis Hanon, translated Theodore Baker, Schirmer's Library of Musical Classics, vol. 925
2 'Pischna Technical Studies, sixty progressive exercises for the piano' by Josef Pischna (composer).
3 For an introduction to Alexander Technique and information see www.alexandertechnique.com.

and feeling a centre of gravity in your heels means that you can sit on the edge of the stool and liberate the whole of your body for use as needs be. It wasn't for nothing that Vladimir Ashkenazy once said that he plays with his feet![4] I like to sit at the piano with my feet slightly splayed but near the pedals, ready for action. I try to keep the lower part of my legs (up to the knees) at a 90° angle to my feet when not pedalling. Alexander Technique teachers usually stress the importance of a straight back that nonetheless preserves the natural curvature of the spine, with the neck a continuation of the line rather than at a new angle.

Effortless expansion

There should be a feeling of 'effortless expansion' about your posture, a sense that as you play, your body becomes more coordinated, more 'at one' with the instrument. You should sense lightness, lack of effort, even a lack of awareness of difficulty. Contracted movements, such as a rounding of the shoulders, bending of the back, movements forward of all kinds and tension in the throat and neck are entirely negative. I would probably include looking down at the keyboard in the category of 'negative contraction', simply because when you are confident enough to look straight ahead things are most certainly 'rolling' in a transcendental sense. In other words, confidence and the desire to listen properly to the sounds coming out of the instrument are triumphing over such mundane matters as 'wrong notes' and mechanical accuracy. (As soon as a pianist starts worrying or even thinking about accuracy, his/her playing immediately becomes more inaccurate and untidy!) When you are performing, only the music matters. Many great artists have described losing awareness of time and technique when they are performing at their very best.

I would suggest that if you feel the need to lower your stool as you continue your practice session then you are experiencing a healthy expansion, with the shoulders opening out in a natural way, the spine lengthening and your neck feeling hollow, free and light. It should be easy for a teacher to move your entire head backwards and forwards effortlessly, with no resistance whatsoever.

4 1960s BBC television interview.

General posture

Comfort and common sense should dictate most other considerations of posture. The distance the seat is placed from the instrument obviously varies depending on size. You are sitting way too far away if your elbows are locked and too near if the angle of your upper and lower arm is less than 90° as you look down. Though pianists vary the angle of their fingers depending on stylistic context, it is interesting to try to pick up a pencil without thinking about it (thumb on one side, four fingers on the other). Notice how curved the fingers are, then transfer that to the keyboard. By so doing you will have a relaxed and natural curve which should be a good starting point. Similarly, you can go a long way to solving hand/wrist position simply by dropping your arms by your sides as you sit at the piano, then flopping them onto the keyboard without pausing to think. Let the force of gravity be your guide! 'Dropping and flopping' is generally the best way to find a natural wrist position, though obviously nothing can be a substitute for a patient and experienced teacher's advice (except your own comfort/pain threshold). Indeed, in all technical considerations it is vital to realise that any discomfort or pain signals from your brain indicate that you are doing something wrong and should stop immediately. If you do not feel natural and comfortable as you play (even in the most demanding passages in the Chopin études) then you are out of control and potentially in trouble. It goes without saying that the old sporting cliché 'no gain without pain' is completely inappropriate in a musical context.

Tension and relaxation

If you were to approach the piano in a completely floppy, spaced-out manner, technical control would of course be impossible. Clearly there ought to be points of intensity and firmness, and the fingertips must be firm and focused at all times. If I were to summarise pianistic problems into a single sentence, it would probably be something like this:

> 'Technical control at the piano can only exist when the performer has achieved complete firmness in the fingertips along with total freedom and relaxation in the wrists, elbows and shoulders.'

As a teacher I spend many hours trying to solve this enormous issue with all of my pupils at some stage, and throughout my practising career it is the thought that I keep foremost in my mind at all times when tackling mechanical difficulties. Though it divorces the thumbs (called 'black sheep' by Vladimir de Pachmann[5]) from consideration, it certainly leads to an immediate reaction as regards stiffness generally. In fact coordination, articulation and freedom at the instrument have been known to improve dramatically once the ability to control yet isolate the fingers has been mastered. For these reasons the importance of the statement above cannot be over-emphasised. Issues of finger

5 From a private conversation with Ronald Stevenson. I am indebted to Stevenson for so many anecdotes about the great pianist-composers. Most of these referred to here come from my own private conversations with Stevenson in his home from April 1983–June 1988.

independence and thumb shifts will be tackled later, but we should begin by stressing that firm finger-tips combined with total freedom is central not only to a solid technical foundation, but also for physical well-being.

Obviously it is easier to cultivate or cure problems with younger rather than older pianists, but if the problem is viewed as a challenge of mental/physical coordination rather than an insurmountable horror, then I do believe that much can be achieved by all – *away* from the keyboard. By practising on desk tops, books or even your own knees it is possible to sort out what is in essence the big pianistic stumbling block. Then we can return to the piano to apply this new coordination skill in a musical context. Try taking each hand in turn, resting it on your knee with a comfortable hand position and slightly curved fingers, then try to feel complete firmness from the knuckles downwards. The two lower joints (anatomically classified as 'distal' and 'proximal interphalangeal' joints respectively) of each of the four fingers should not be allowed to collapse, and there should be a feeling of firmness and oneness running from the knuckles ('metacarpophalangeal' joints) to each fingertip:

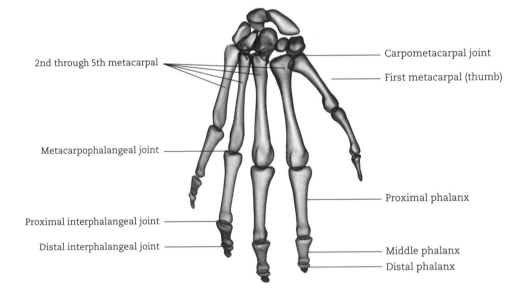

Ronan O'Hora[6] discusses the sensation of gripping the keys 'as though you were gripping the edge of a cliff, with a 1,000 foot drop below'.

As you examine each hand in turn, you can help by massaging your opposite wrist with small circular movements in each direction, to 'de-block' any stiffness which may be present. Elbow joints, neck, shoulders and shoulder blades should also be checked with the opposite hand so that they remain free with a sensation of lightness.

Many students, even advanced pianists, find it impossible to achieve this along with firmness in their fingertips. When they relax, their fingers collapse, but when firm, they become tense everywhere. As in all technical considerations,

6 Ronan O'Hora's performance classes at Chetham's School of Music, 1997–98.

patience has to be the rule, however progress often comes when one least expects it. Significant progress has been known to occur when individuals have abstained from all practice and been away from pianos for several weeks!

Exercises and warm-ups

Having mentioned Hanon at the beginning of this first chapter, it is only fair to conclude with the suggestion that 'de-blocking' wrist work could be continued at the keyboard via the first twenty exercises from the celebrated master's volume.

If a student is able to cope with firm fingers and free wrists on his knee or table, it is logical to try to get the same results via Hanon. This can be in small sections, *mezzo piano*, stopping for breaks every five notes, whilst at all times observing, thinking, reviewing and listening. Eventually each Hanon exercise can be played with fewer and fewer pauses, with stronger dynamics and the metronome marking more adventurous. All of this counts for very little without a firm foundation of knowledge and understanding and in order to achieve these we will examine basic approaches, principles and considerations in the next few chapters.

At all stages in technical development, 'mini-breaks' should be taken in practise sessions. By that I mean short walks round the room as well as 'arm flops' whereby each arm is dropped and held loose by your sides until an awareness of tingles in the fingertips is obvious[7]. We all know the feeling of swollen fingers after long walks, and one of the dangers of piano playing is that our hands are constantly raised in an unnatural way. They are not given the chance to drop, and are therefore deprived of as surging a flow of blood as they get when aerobic exercise is undertaken. Try 'arm flopping' for good circulation every five minutes or so at first and you cannot go wrong!

Finally, the importance of a calm, regular warm-up routine should be stressed for every player at any level. I would advise that part of the warm-up should consist of standing with a sensible posture away from the piano, then transferring that to the stool at the instrument. You should never attempt to play with cold hands, and a good way to instil firm finger-work with free wrists is to start your daily practice by playing a sequence of eight- to ten-note chords quietly, checking posture and wrist and hand positions. Each chord should be securely gripped yet completely comfortable and effortless. I recommend that a 'cooling down' period at the end of the day is advisable, whereby the warm-up process is repeated.[8]

Pianists who find it difficult to tackle new technical approaches may find it necessary to play the piano on two different levels: the 'ideal', whereby they strive for perfection in their technical exercises, and the 'old', whereby inevitably some of their bad habits come back as they work on repertoire or play through repertoire at sight. Though much harm can be done by wearing

7 See Appendix 1 exercise 1
8 Ibid

two proverbial hats, it is often too extreme to tell individuals to stop playing all repertoire for six months until technical issues are resolved. Progress usually has to be undertaken in such a manner that the technically 'ideal' approach only gradually connects with the 'old' approach, even if there is an obvious flow, over a period of time, from the latter into the former.

Encouragement and sympathy from all around the pianist is essential, especially for those over a certain age. So here, at the beginning of what may well be new technical challenges, overhauls and approaches, it is especially important to be positively patient, as well as focused and energised. Technique at the piano takes time to cultivate and nurture.

Lifestyle warm-ups away from the piano

Yoga, transcendental meditation, visualisation, breathing exercises, Alexander Technique, Feldenkrais exercises in movement and t'ai chi have, in their completely different ways, proved that they can cause positive transformations for practising musicians. Finding which ones are best suited to your own taste and temperament may be a case of trial and error, but the time spent will never be wasted.

Whatever you choose, it is important to stay in good physical shape. Hiring a personal trainer could be a good investment, especially if you are given a series of appropriate stretching exercises to tackle as a sensible prelude to piano exercises.[9]

Visualisation in advance of the practice session you are about to embark on is equally important. It can mean all the difference between a positive experience and a completely frustrating one. As technique is about putting into practice what one wishes to deliver, it is vital that you also take time before playing to articulate in your mind exactly what it is you are trying to achieve.

Creative warm-ups at the keyboard

Sound quality and variety of touch/tone must remain the top priorities in all of your work. I enjoy playing solitary notes at different dynamic levels and also slow chords when first approaching the piano each day. Simply highlighting each note in an eight-part chord in turn immediately opens up your ears, which will demand that your body responds with subtle shifts in weight and balance in order to emphasise each note of the chord. (See appendix 1 for suggested daily warm-up exercises that cover most of the essential issues discussed in the opening chapters of this book.)

---

9 See www.warmupsandstretchesforpianists.wordpress.com by Tom Hicks for useful daily exercises.

2 Alignment

'Perhaps there is nothing more dangerous in piano playing than poor wrist-arm alignment.'

At the exact moment keys are struck, anything other than a straight line from the wrist through the lower arm to the elbow is clearly unhealthy. The angle of this straight line in relation to the keyboard will vary considerably as you play, and it is worth remembering that undulating movements of the wrist *in between* notes are vital for preparation and relaxation. These should resemble sine waves (or if you want to be more childlike, Loch Ness monster shapes!). However, the alignment rule for the wrist and arm must always apply at the actual moment when a note resonates. Anything else indicates that your tendons are being stretched, which at the very least means that playing is more of a strain than it should be.

This picture shows good arm-wrist alignment at a 0° angle with the keyboard:

The two pictures below show poor alignment. In the first the wrist is dangerously low, and in the second both wrists are too high:

I recommend that you set up a mirror at the side of your piano, and that you spend time observing your arm-wrist alignment whilst practising. Take time to adjust so that you have sufficient space and freedom in order to produce a straight line from your wrist to elbow when you play. This may involve consideration of the stool height, your elbows (frequently students keep them too close to their sides) and shoulders. But the crucial anatomical parts here are the wrists.

This famous picture of Johannes Brahms seated at the piano may surprise some in terms of the high 30-45° angle that his arms adopt (just how high is Brahms' piano stool?). For our purposes here the picture is very helpful. Even though Brahms' left wrist and arm are unaligned because of the crossing hands manoeuvre he is evidently engaged in, his right arm and wrist show a perfect straight line – an excellent aligned approach from above the keyboard.

Clearly this is a good illustration of natural ease at the piano, which is achieved through relaxation rather than by strained tension. In order to eliminate the latter, begin with arm exercises away from the piano. Walking around the room and swinging your arms freely in the style of a chimpanzee is a good starting point. Next, stand in a splayed but firmly anchored feet position and swing your arms separately, then together, in bigger and bigger movements from your shoulders. Feel complete lightness and ease in both arms as you do this. When you go to the piano to work, it is important to stop and 'drop' your arms to recapture this sensation of light ease. It is also important not to 'lock' your arms into your side. As the pianist and teacher John Gough once commented in an open lesson in Manchester: 'give your armpits plenty of fresh air!'[10] Indeed, a relaxed mobility, flexibility and swivelling or 'rotary' movement from the elbows is not only healthy to practise – it can also remove countless technical problems. How sad to remember that in past generations students were often firmly told to keep their elbows still and close to their sides.

10 John Gough's 'open' piano lesson at Chetham's School of Music, 2010.

In order to move these ideas forward, play five adjacent notes simultaneously in each hand on the keyboard using all your fingers. Keep your hands two or three octaves apart (choose whichever notes you wish). Keep the notes firmly pressed down, but experiment with raising the arms upwards then downwards, keeping arm alignment consistent throughout.

It may be necessary to adjust both the height of your stool as well as the distance it is positioned from the piano in order to achieve convincing alignment. Shoulders should not rise as you do this, though of course elbows may. Give yourself plenty of space at the instrument, and aim for a straight back without rigidity (i.e. do not try to eliminate the natural curve in your lower spine by sitting artificially upright, with tension holding your position in place). Lightness and ease of movement must be consistently aimed for. Imagine that each arm is like a taut but never over-stretched rope that is hung over a valley from two mountain tops (your fingertips are one 'mountain' whilst your shoulder is the other). There should be a sense of controlled relaxation as you continue exercises by gently rotating in clockwise, then anti-clockwise movements from your elbows. Whilst doing this you should take care to avoid stiffness and tension in your neck. Indeed, your whole body should feel free and weightless. It should be as though the gentle suppleness and freedom that develops from your arms stimulates relaxation and lightness everywhere else in your anatomy.

3 Finger independence

> 'True finger independence for pianists means using each digit in turn without any movement from the others in the same hand. It is a vital basic skill.'

Our ten digits require constant attention from the earliest stages to the most advanced levels of technical development. No matter how relaxed, coordinated, creative, imaginative and prepared at the instrument a pianist is, faulty articulation and lack of expertise from the knuckles downwards usually means insecurity, lack of control and frustration all round.

Over the years Hanon's exercises have traditionally been prescribed to those with weak fingers as a suitable remedy. I remember many years ago, a much-loved teacher telling a new student after their first lesson to practise the first twenty exercises from Hanon with high finger work in every key, inching up the metronome from crotchet = 60 to 112, and to do so for at least an hour a day, 'until your fingers ache':

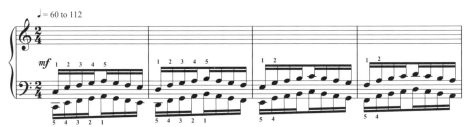

Hanon: *The Virtuoso Pianist*, exercise 1

This approach is close to the old concept of 'playing through the pain' which was possibly inspired by certain sports masters from the past which we now realise can lead to serious (even permanent) injury. I believe this is totally unacceptable as an approach for musicians. An introduction to piano technique like this from a teacher today would be severely frowned upon by BAPAM[11], and could lead to litigation in our increasingly injury conscious politically correct era. For these reasons, 21st-century piano tutors would be wise to encourage a warm-up and cool-down routine for all pupils, as suggested in Chapter 1, along with general fitness recommendations and schedules that allow a pianist to improve their coordination, stamina and strength gradually.

It is important to begin finger training in a relaxed and intelligent manner, remembering that a real mastery of technique comes from mental coordination,

11   See www.bapam.org.uk: British Association for Performing Arts Medicine.

focus and intellectual awareness rather than from mindless physical repetition. You should simply ignore the instructions at the beginning of Hanon's exercises to lift your fingers high as you play all the semiquavers which proliferate his famous exercises.

Effective modern-day piano pedagogy encourages students to listen acutely not only to their practice, but also to their bodies. Physical discomfort of any description is a useful 'alarm bell' warning that things are not working as healthily as they should be. Let's consider a more comfortable, less brutally athletic alternative way forward for our fingers.

Touch and press

Hanon's suggestion that 'fingers should be lifted high' is a guaranteed way of creating tension and stiffness in your wrists. By attacking the keys with your ten digits, you are doing everything possible to be percussive: you are quite literally hammering the piano! It is infinitely healthier and more musically appealing to prepare your articulation by resting fingers on the keys before you articulate each note. 'Touch and press' is a beautiful, relaxed approach to piano technique and if shown to a student from lesson one it is possible for a singing tone to be cultivated immediately. Develop 'touch and press' on a daily basis by placing all your fingers on the keyboard in the five-finger position and imagining that each fingertip has been glued down on the keys. Without lifting the fingers, practise producing sounds with each note in turn.

Finger independence from the 'touch and press' approach is vital for evenness, control, economy of movement and ease with a whole range of technical challenges, including double notes and trills. When other fingers move whilst you are trilling, the result is more cumbersome than if they do not. If your fifth finger lifts when you are playing your second and third, you are carrying unnecessary tension, straining your hand and so carrying an uncomfortable burden. You are certainly not realising your full technical potential.

Perhaps most serious of all is the inability to keep non-playing fingers quiet in Mozartian scalic passages (scales in both hands simultaneously) leading to frustration and angst. In this context accents and bumps can seem impossible to remove and no matter how much practice is done, students will never be able to play evenly until they have mastered the ability to separate each finger with ease.

Independence of fingers

True finger independence means using each digit in turn without any movement from the others in the same hand. It is a vital basic skill. Though there are talented youngsters around who seem to have inherited the attribute of finger independence effortlessly (and therefore can manage it with no practice or thought), sadly its absence is usually the norm. It is all too common to witness finger work from students in which their whole hand seems riddled with stiffness. Fingers move in groups rather than individually from one note to the next, resulting in the playing sounding lumpy, unreliable and effortful.

Many technical manuals begin with chapters devoted to independence of the fingers, the implication being that a daily dose of five-finger exercises will lead to perfectly coordinated finger-work, even passagework, neat articulation and precision. Controversially, some volumes imply that the student should strive towards an equalisation of the fingers so that trills between the weaker fourth and fifth fingers become as easy to handle as trills between the second and third or first and second.

As each finger has its own particular colour, strength and personality, it is surely undesirable to aim for a blanket spread of uniformity across the two hands. Instead, it would be better to think of finger independence work as the means by which the student gradually develops an individual personality and creative qualities in each finger.

Choices of fingering can then be made depending on the particular colour the pianist wishes to obtain for a passage.

Finger separation

The actual 'separation' of the fingers is as much a mental exercise as a physical one, and before plunging into such reputable tomes as Beringer[12] or Hanon, I would strongly recommend work on the following brief but succinct scale fragment, each hand separately:

- Place your five fingers over the first five notes of the E major scale so that each finger rests silently on the notes.

- In the right hand: thumb on E above middle C, 2 on F sharp, 3 on G sharp, 4 on A, 5 on B.

- In the left hand: thumb on B below middle C, 2 on A, 3 on G sharp, 4 on F sharp, 5 on E.

Thumb separation

Start the exercise with the thumb of the right hand, and play the note from its resting position on E: do not lift off before playing the note. Keep repeating it, constantly making sure that the other four fingers do not move. Trembles, collapsing joints, slight moves downwards of the keys and strange angular movements from the non-performing fingers are all strictly forbidden. The zero tolerance approach to avoiding key depression should be observed. There should be a feeling of 'separation' of the thumb, as though an infra-red light is beaming down from your brain into the fleshy pad of the thumb, making it play effortlessly while the wrist remains supple, the neck and shoulders light, and the arms and elbows free.

It is always important to consider curvature and non-curvature of the fingers when you place them on the keys. Flat-fingered pianism has its place, especially in the high Romantic repertoire where indulgence with *legato* and depth of sound are prerequisites. Though there is a natural, instinctive curvature (you can find this by picking up a pencil without thinking about it), it is fascinating to note how the sound can change depending on how curved or flat your fingers are.

Always remember that the thumb has three joints (not two – beware of missing the joint nearest the wrist!) and all three should remain as light, free of stiffness and as relaxed as possible in this first exercise. This should remain the norm for all your playing. As you practise, do ensure that your posture is set up as described in Chapter 1 and you should remain calm, patient and take regular breaks throughout finger-independence work.

Separating the fingers

After mastering the art of separating the thumb from the rest of the hand consider the slightly harder task of separating the first finger. Repeat the exercise on F sharp with your index digit, making sure that the rest of your fingers remain stationary. Each finger should feel firm from the knuckles (the 'bridge') downwards, with the lower joints working in synchronisation from the bridge downwards as one single unit.

Next is the G sharp (finger 3) then A (4) and finally B (5), before the same thing is repeated with the left hand on its own. I recommend only a few minutes of concentrated effort at a time for those who are struggling (unfortunately it tends to be adults rather than children who find this especially daunting). Students generally find that for some time they have two distinct levels of pianism: the independent level for their exercises, and a less coordinated approach when they return to play repertoire. Gradually the repertoire level will merge with the level adopted in the exercises.

Developing finger independence

Now that we have managed to separate each finger in isolation, I recommend playing the five notes in succession (E-F sharp-G sharp-A-B), still keeping all digits stuck on the keys, allowing absolutely no movement other than the note being played at the time. Incidentally, E major rather than C major is recommended because in the latter key the second and third fingers are a little too cramped. Try the five notes in succession non-*legato*, then *staccato*, then *legato*.

For *legato* it will be necessary to isolate each individual stage in the process. In other words for the right hand:

1 Depress E with thumb.

2 Continue to hold the E down as you depress F sharp with your index finger.

3 Lift up thumb, keeping it 'stuck' on the E.

4 Continue to keep down your index finger as you depress G sharp with your middle finger, etc.

The finger-independence principle can be extended by using arm movement, (more on weight in Chapter 5) or by raising the fingers before each note is played. I find the most useful continuations are trill-based in triplets. Continue to feel as though your five fingers have been literally glued to the keys as you play trills on the first five notes of E major for each finger in turn:

Right hand

Left hand

Right hand

Left hand

Patience remains the key for success and if the double-third exercise exposes a lack of co-ordination much progress can be made away from the instrument simply by practising on work tops, knees or just by thinking over the challenges. When this exercise is mastered it can be extended further by using different keys and different fingerings.

Achieving success in exercises

Chapter 1 in Alfred Cortot's 'Rational Principles of Piano Technique'[13] contains extremely challenging exercises, or at least they are challenging if executed with absolutely no movement from non-playing fingers. Here lies one of the great pitfalls with exercises generally: exercises are only useful if they are studied with intelligence and understanding. They can be pointless and physically damaging if approached in the wrong manner and for this reason it is always best to study them with help from a teacher aware of the technical requirements of the exercises in question.

Apart from improving the smoothness, precision and accuracy of your playing, finger independence makes life easier. It helps to eliminate unwanted tension and is also aesthetically beautiful to look at. In this context I always think of Vladimir Ashkenazy's television broadcasts of Beethoven sonatas a number of years ago[14]. During the extremely taxing demands of the last sonatas the camera focused on the maestro's hands, revealing a remarkable lack of unnecessary movement and an almost childlike technical ease. Little wonder that this particular artist is so renowned for his outstanding handling of double notes (witness his recordings of Liszt's 'Feux Follets' and Chopin's Étude Op.25 No.6).

The technique of double notes, and indeed the technique of polyphonic playing, will have to wait as the main concern here has been to establish good practice which can be thought through and worked on each day, whether you are a pre-grade one pupil or a post-graduate student at a conservatoire.

Let's close this chapter with some anecdotes for stimulation and encouragement as you toil towards economic coordination:

Vladimir Horowitz's right-hand fifth finger was far from 'independent' throughout his famous Moscow recital in 1986. In fact it was riddled with

13   Alfred Cortot: 'Rational Principles of Piano Technique', 1928 (Salabert)
14   Christopher Nupen's films of Ashkenazy performances can be seen on www.medici.tv showing Ashkenazy's impressive finger independence in the second movement of Beethoven's Sonata in E, Op.109.

tension and sticking up for most of the concert, even if he still played like the genius he was!

At the other end of the spectrum, finger independence may have prevented Frank Merrick from ending up in hospital a number of years ago when he accompanied Dame Clara Butt in Australia, with a bumble bee on his head during one of the songs! Economy of movement and trust in his superlative technical control meant that this wonderful composer-performer-pedagogue was able to stay still and so allow the minibeast freedom to explore the terrains of his bald patch without either party becoming unduly anxious.

Back in Victorian drawing rooms, it was not uncommon to see young ladies practising with farthings on the backs of their hands, the belief being that if they fell off, the non-playing fingers were not sufficiently still. Horrific as the implications for tension are in this concept, Harold Schonberg in 'The Great Pianists' mentions that it was a technique particularly utilised by Muzio Clementi in his teaching.[15]

15 Harold Schonberg refers to the coins that Clementi used to place on the top of his star pupil John Field's hand to prevent movement during their lessons. He also mentions Liszt's reminiscences of Field performing with remarkably still hands in Paris (see Harold C. Schonberg 'The Great Pianists', Victor Gollancz, London 1964).

4 The thumb

'If you have thumb independence then your whole technique can be stabilised.'

The great pianist and legendary eccentric Vladimir de Pachmann was not being outlandish when he frequently complained in public about his thumbs.[16] On the contrary, the two thumbs, or 'naughty children' as some would have us believe, can cause technical havoc if left unattended and undisciplined. Unwanted accents in mid phrase, split notes, bumps on position shifts and lack of security often stem from poor thumb control, so it is vital that particular individual care is given to these digits.

Thumb joints

As mentioned in Chapter 3, thumbs have three joints, labelled clearly in the diagram showing finger and thumb joints below. The first joint, the one closest to the keyboard is called the 'interphalangeal' joint. The middle one is the 'metacarpophalangeal' joint, and the third, biggest one is the 'carpometacarpal' joint. It is crucial that they work freely and naturally when playing the piano.

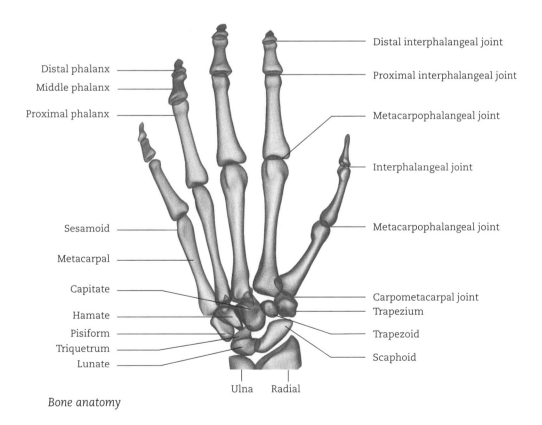

Bone anatomy

16 Private conversations with Ronald Stevenson, 1983 8 ibid

To avoid blocking thumb movements with stiffness and tension, draw miniature clockwise and anti-clockwise circles in the air with each thumb away from the piano to liberate thumb movement.

As a teacher with many years' experience working with some outstanding talents, I have yet to come across a student who did not come to me initially for lessons *without* stiffness in their thumb joints. Indeed, it is fair to say that the majority of pupils are unaware that each hand actually owns more than two thumb joints in the first place. The process of getting pupils to lighten and mobilise their thumbs tends to be time consuming and even frustrating but it is an essential technical hurdle to overcome.

Thumbing under

Here are some simple *legato* 'thumbing under' triadic exercises (also useful later when we consider changing position and introducing arpeggio work in Chapters 7 and 10) which can accelerate healthy development if combined with constant experimentation away from the piano (e.g. locking and unlocking the joints and gently massaging each joint in turn with the other hand).

Practise a–c hands separately and together.

(a) Start with right hand only, using 1 and 3 on C and E. As soon as E sounds, begin to slide your thumb upwards in preparation for the G. Reverse this process in descent, sliding your thumb under as soon as the E has sounded in preparation for the final note. For the left hand, reverse the notes in contrary motion, starting with G below middle C.

(b) Slide your thumb along the keyboard as much as possible (think 'slugs and slime' not 'kangaroos and bunny hops'). The wrist will have to move upwards and downwards slightly more than in (a), and it will not be possible for students with short thumbs to keep touching the keyboard at all times. Reverse the notes in contrary motion for the left hand.

(c) The elbow becomes more involved, and only those with exceptionally large thumbs and highly developed flexibility will be able to keep their thumbs touching the keys at all times.

Relaxed movements

Convincing *legato* changes of thumb position involve concentrated yet relaxed movements. It is essential to master these rudimentary 'thumbing-under' exercises before proceeding with authority towards scales and arpeggios, though arguably (c) demands more flexibility than is strictly necessary for even the most awkward of arpeggios in grade examination syllabuses. Regular work on these exercises and their transposed variations will certainly develop vital independence of thumb movement. If you have thumb independence then your whole technique can be stabilised. Your thumbs can rest on the keyboard for long stretches of demanding passagework, providing firm anchorage for your hands.

Every pianist's thumbs are different, and whilst it can be easy for those with supple joints and large fingers to keep their thumbs 'on point', by remaining permanently glued to the keyboard throughout the big cadenza of Rachmaninov's third concerto, players with smaller hands who are more prone to physical tension will need to be more pragmatic. Thumb nightmares to avoid are the 'kangaroo' syndrome, with thumbs in air-born mode, and stiffness (remember that the thumb's three joints all need to be supple and relaxed).

There are subtle movements of the wrist, lower arm and elbow involved in position shifts (most of which are far easier to demonstrate than to write about), and some pedagogues insist that their students buy yo-yos and such like so that they can get their wrists to work correctly. Changing position will be explored in more detail later. Meanwhile the emphasis here is on comfort and concentration of movement at all times when moving the thumb.

During and after thumb conversion, nothing less than complete freedom of movement should be accepted. If this leads to short-term frustration and nothing but slow 'stuck in a rut' work for a few weeks then it is all for a worthy cause. Eventually pennies do drop and without eliminating thumb tension life as a pianist is simply too hard. After conversion, scale passagework in particular can transform from a quasi-Latin American mess of cross accents (caused by clumsy thumb shifts resulting in unwanted accents) into elegant effortlessness, with the listener unaware of thumb usage. 'Thumbs should be seen but not heard' seems an appropriate maxim to suggest at this stage, as indeed is the idea that less rather than more thumb shifts are nearly always to be preferred when fingering.

Thumb resonance

The thumb is capable of tremendous richness and resonance of tone. With full arm weight and 'touch and press' coordination behind it in a totally relaxed approach, it becomes a sensuous implement capable of enormous expressive powers. Always play with the fleshy side of the thumb rather than the tip, and begin exploring by imagining the thumb glued to one of the keys. Slowly depress a note with this 'glued aesthetic' in mind. Repeat this single note many times, slowly, allowing each tone to envelope itself into the next. Feel the sonority coming through from your upper arm, shoulder and back as it gets deeper and more 'organic' with each stoke:

Use lots of pedal in the early stages, then gradually use less until you can play with no pedal at all.

When this sonority test has been mastered, extend the exercise by playing single note scales with the thumb alone, aiming to hide all gaps. Aim to create an illusion of perfect *legato* as the decay of each note's tone 'drawls' itself reluctantly into the opening sounds of the next note:

The many excellent thumb exercises in Alfred Cortot's 'Rational Principles of Piano Technique'[17] utilise and develop this approach and demand total freedom and concentration of coordination from the executant.

Further thumb development

On a less artistic plane it is well worth developing a more literal physical over-lapping technique for single notes from the thumb, using the interphalangeal joint (the one nearest to the keyboard) as a pivot device. By leaning with this joint on the first note, you can reach out and depress the note that follows with the tip of your thumb, then move your interphalangeal joint over to catch the next note to be played. This can all be done with overlaps between the notes.

Begin with an exercise. Use your interphalangeal thumb joint as a pivot to play a *legato* C major scale in each hand:

Literal overlapping thumb notes, pivoting on the thumb joint nearest the keyboard.

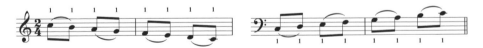

Next, try connecting the C to B natural (left hand) in bar three of the first movement of Beethoven's 'Appassionata' Sonata:

There are countless examples in the literature which will benefit enormously from this *legato* connection.

Thumb stability

The thumb has a pivotal role to play in non-*legato* and *staccato* octave passages. In these contexts you should feel firmness in the part of the thumb which makes contact with the keys. In octave arpeggios in particular, the thumb can usefully be thought of as a metaphorical 'handle' for the trolley, which is the hand as a whole, as it travels across the keyboard touching every key as it moves (this is called lateral movement and will be discussed later). This is a 'sliding' thumb technique in which all notes are touched (naturally without allowing notes to sound) by the thumb as it travels up and down the keyboard.

Thumbs can vary enormously from one hand to the next, and though some students find it impossible to keep contact with the keyboard consistently in *legato* passages, I believe that the ideal of exploring maximum thumb-keyboard contact throughout the whole repertoire is extremely worthwhile. Those with large hands will find it possible to maintain thumb contact with the keyboard in most contexts (provided they are supple and flexible enough in their wrists elbows and arms) and will discover that the thumb can act as a tremendous stabiliser for all passagework, particularly when it is not playing. Those with shorter thumbs need to remain as close to the keyboard as is comfortably possible, and think in terms of horizontal, economical shifts from position to position.

It seems somewhat ironic that silent thumbs can be so useful to the overall technical grasp of a performance (or indeed so destructive if they remain airborne or stiff). Speed and coordination of fast 'sliding under' movements needs to be mastered to the very highest level, and for this I recommend that students practise (hands separately in slow tempo and in small segments at a time) Chopin's F major Etude Op.10 No.8 (for the right hand) and the C minor 'Revolutionary' Etude (for the left). If proper analytical attention over an extended period is given to thumb movement in these two studies, much can be achieved of lasting value to virtually every possible pianistic hurdle encountered in the literature.

To conclude: keep your thumbs touching the keyboard for as long as you can. Resist the temptation to remove them from the instrument. Thumbs can act as invaluable stabilisers for the fingers. If they are harnessed and disciplined into position they can change from being the proverbial 'black sheep' of the hands into protective, stabilising shepherds that provide a welcome sense of security and protection for the fingers they guide.

5 Touches: part 1

Non-*legato*, weight and lateral movement

> 'Coordination and understanding may take time, but when successful the resulting warmth of sonority and ease of execution will make the frustrations of practice well worth it.'

For the purposes of getting started on the enormous subject of touch, let's identify non-*legato*, *staccato* and *legato* as the three basic touch families. Within each category there is infinite variety. As we are dealing with mechanical foundations, classifications will be made technically rather than by imaginative association (as is often done in mid-flow by especially charismatic pedagogues).

Arm weight

The basic principles and exercises shown in Chapter 3 will make it easy for you to get started with coordinated non-*legato* playing. Place right hand fingers 1–5 on middle C–G. Repeat each note four times in turn without lifting the particular finger off the key in between each repetition. This is a basic 'arm weight' non-*legato* touch which should feel effortless and comfortable if the considerations regarding posture and freedom in Chapters 1 and 2 are adhered to.

Arm weight is a vital approach for minimising effort in performance in that it takes the effort away from your fingers and has a profoundly positive effect on the quality of your sound production. If you silently prepare notes by touching them in advance with your fingers, playing them without lifting your fingers off the keys, you are using upper arm weight. It is possible to feel all of the energy and impetus for articulation coming from this weight rather than from the knuckles and wrists. I would argue that this approach more than any other can lead to a healthy technique and one in which stamina ceases to be an issue at all.

By experimenting with bigger and smaller leverage of the arm it is possible to vary arm-weight tone, creating a range of sound from *leggiero* to *molto pesante*. Arm leverage experimentation also makes it possible to improve coordination. Strive for perfect synchronisation (the arm-wrist alignment examined in Chapter 2) between the moment the key 'speaks' and the point at which the arm-wrist reaches its lowest point (which should form a straight line in parallel to the floor).

Experience has shown that students new to playing with arm weight often cannot synchronise finger and arm-wrist movements, producing poor alignment with strange, ungainly strokes in which the finger often plays whilst the wrist is still high. Breakthroughs in work will occur when the student is able to realise that (in arm weight), it should feel as though the upper arm, rather than the finger, is playing the note, and therefore the finger should be thought of as an extension of the arm, rather than as a separate entity. Once single-note work has been mastered, try playing triads, four-note chords and octaves with arm weight. Coordination and understanding may take time, but when successful the resulting warmth of sonority and ease of execution will make the frustrations of practice well worth it.

Non-*legato* playing

There is more variety involved in non-*legato* playing than what is obtainable by mere leverage of the arm-wrist. It is fascinating to experiment with non-*legato* playing by specifically identifying **six** different perspectives from which it is possible to play. Each perspective has its own particular character and colour, and can be subjected to enormous variation in terms of leverage, from the very smallest angle to the largest 'backswings' which are comfortable. For the sake of lucidity, let's stick with right-hand fingers 1–5 placed again over middle C-G , and focus on the index finger as it repeats D over and over again, with different emphasis on each repetition:

1. Firstly think of the **knuckle** as the pivot point. Forget everything behind the knuckle (wrist, arm, shoulder and trunk) and imagine that it is only the finger and the knuckle that are involved with sound production. Beginning with the finger resting on the D, lift it up ('backswing' it) by a few millimetres, then play. Immediately 'backswing' again, but go slightly higher this time. Keep the two lower joints of the finger absolutely firm as you continue to increase the leverage of each backswing. The speed of descent should also increase, producing a steady *crescendo* of non-*legato* pianism from the knuckles. The sound should be *martellato* (literally hammered and detached), which has its place in all kinds of musical contexts (though obviously not in a Chopin nocturne!).

The next five pivot centres should be tried with the index finger constantly glued to D (i.e. both whilst playing and between each stroke):

2. Focus on the **wrist**, and forget everything behind it. Imagine that it is the wrist's descending movement which produces the sonority of each repeated D. It may be useful to grasp the wrist with the third finger and thumb of your left hand as you practise small backswings at the keyboard followed by actual non-*legato* strokes downwards in which the index finger's movement is kept to a minimum. Gradually the angles of the repeated backstrokes should widen as the sonority and speed of execution increases. At all times care should be taken not to stiffen or tighten. Indeed, breaks in which the whole arm is allowed to flop down loosely are strongly recommended.

3. Continue this anatomical coordination exercise by taking the **elbow** joint as the pivot point (or proverbial 'door hinge'), followed by the (4) **shoulder** then (5) the **lower back**. Finally, it is amusing to feel your (6) **feet** as the pivot point. If you sit on the edge of the stool and feel (as you should do) that your feet rather

than your seat supports your body as you play, then it is comparatively easy to rise off the stool and coordinate the highest point of your 'ascent' with the impact of playing a note, chord or octave.

The body is moving towards the instrument when this exercise is working well, but when it comes to actual performing and playing in a musical context I find that it is much more effective, refined and less superficial not to jump about. Feeling the sonority from one's lower back and feet is what is important in massive passage work, and though wild leaps off the piano stool always make for good theatre, in practice they usually have the effect of dissipating energy and actually reducing the amount of tone overall.

When it comes to putting non-*legato* into practice it will probably be found that the upper arm is useful as the point of leverage in slower tempos where there is time to prepare notes by covering them with fingers in advance of attack. Slow, weighted non-*legato* scale work in this mode makes for an excellent warm-up. More brilliant, percussive sonorities demand strokes from the knuckles, and much time and effort needs to be spent in gradually building up a motoric digital facility in which reliability is dependent on loose wrists, with no arm movement behind them.

Practice on work tops is useful here in the early stages, and velocity of finger movement needs to be accelerated gradually to the point at which the five fingers can play C-G and back again in an effortless tonal cascade. Think of what happens when you line up a deck of cards back to back then gently push the card at the end of the row: fingers need to move as effortlessly and inevitably as this, with no joint collapses, and if that means an intense blitz on the first twenty exercises in Hanon's much-mentioned 'Virtuoso Pianist',[18] then so be it. Tell your friends and family to run for cover as you gradually build up velocity via the metronome! Increase the speed of each Hanon study patiently in turn and the results will be of lasting benefit.

Changing position with non-*legato* touch: lateral movement

The most effective and healthy method of changing position when adopting a non-*legato* touch is through lateral movement. Lateral movement occurs when the hand, wrist and lower arm move together as one unit from side to side across the keyboard. This is a crucial technique to develop for octaves, chords, *staccato* and non-*legato* passagework and leaps, for it ensures the economical coordinated movement of the hand-wrist-arm as one effective tool. Without mastery of lateral movement, it is impossible to really move effectively and comfortably over the keyboard.

For non-*legato* octave and chordal passages, try thinking of the hand as one entity, rather like a supermarket trolley, with the keyboard as the proverbial 'food-aisle' over which the trolley travels. Your wrist must always remain parallel to the keyboard as your hands move up and down from right to left,

18 Hanon. Ibid

and back again. For the inexperienced, lateral movement can be a rather bewildering technique to conquer, as it takes time for the hand to learn how to remain absolutely still whilst the arm and wrist carry it around. Begin work by practising lateral movement away from the piano. Stand and hold your arm out in a straight line in front of your body. Allow your arm to slowly move your (constantly still and quiet) hand first to the right side and then to the left of your body. Feel as though your hand is completely dead and that your arm is gently but firmly guiding it along an imaginary line in the air.

Return to the piano and imagine your hand again as a supermarket trolley and the 'food aisle' is the keyboard over which the trolley is pushed (see Appendix 1, ex. 7). Depending on the technical and musical context, the trolley should be thought of as moving in the following ways, all of which should be practised on a work top, rather than at the keyboard, until complete coordination is assured:

(a) **Thumb emphasised as the leader** (the handle of the trolley). Grasp the thumb of your right hand with your left and glide your right hand smoothly up and down a worktop, stopping after varying distances as if to fill your basket with goodies, but constantly keeping the hand concentrated as one static entity. Next, transfer this process to the piano and silently glide up and down the keys, keeping your wrist, elbow, arm and shoulder as light and free of stiffness as possible. Repeat the process for the left hand.

(b) **Hand emphasis**: repeat (a), but lightly grasp your wrist with your other hand, now viewing this as the handle of the trolley rather than your thumb. Go through the whole process of (a), only transferring the exercise to the keyboard from your worktop when coordination and ease is achieved.

(c) **Elbow as leader**: this time the elbow is grasped and viewed as the handle of the trolley. Go through the usual process in full before proceeding.

(d) **Upper arm**: feel centred and controlled technically from the upper part of your arm, so that your whole side seems to move from just below your shoulder joint.

These exercises are invaluable for non-*legato* movements around the instrument and need to be applied also to *staccato* passagework. Holistically, they help students towards improved co-ordination, giving them a stronger awareness of suppleness and freedom.

6 Touches: part 2

Staccato and the development of reflexes

'Working at *staccato* techniques is extremely important for developing reflexes and dexterity.'

An effective *staccato* technique needs economy and concentration of both movement and thought. Sadly it is all too common to encounter students with stiff, un-coordinated and uneven *staccato* techniques. Often heaviness and tension makes it impossible to distinguish any difference between a pianist's non-*legato* and *staccato* passagework. Development in this area takes time, patience and coordination. It can prove a frustrating process if left for too long and this is unfortunately often the case, as many teachers refuse to teach *staccato* in the earliest stages. From certain viewpoints this is understandable as major examination boards do not require scales to be played with *staccato* articulation until after grade 5.[19]

Staccato playing

Teachers often seem rather hostile to *staccato* for various reasons. They mention that *legato* playing is essential in order to make the piano 'sing' and that *staccato* playing is in many ways contrary to this, causing stiffness and tension. I would argue that *staccato* as a basic touch is required in the easiest of pieces in the earliest grades, and is easily mastered when tackled sooner rather than later. Stiffness and tension can be avoided in *staccato* playing through good monitoring from the teacher and intelligent awareness from the student.

In most technical work, progress is best made through small sessions of daily practice rather than with irregular marathon stints of work. Economy and concentration of movement are essential in this technique. When playing *staccato* try not to move your entire arm on every note, focus on your fingertips, before analysing how *staccato* can be effectively achieved. It is worth mentioning that there are all kinds of different *staccato* touches in the repertoire, from the most delicate *leggiero* sounds in Mozart through to the heaviest, detached but resonant sounds in Brahms and later composers. We need to adjust our technical set-up in order to cope with stylistic demands and with this in mind it is useful to identify and work at three major *staccato* families from the earliest stages of work:

19   See ABRSM piano grade syllabus requirements at www.abrsm.ac.uk

Close staccato

Let's begin with '**close** *staccato*', when the fingers do not actually move from the keys. Obviously the pianist needs to develop effective hand-position changes before close *staccato* can be used in repertoire (moving fingers as groups on the keys, up to 4 or 5 notes at a time, so that they are in position in advance of execution). Begin work on this touch by placing your ten fingers over ten notes on the keyboard, adopting the approach used in the first exercise of Chapter 3. Imagine your fingers are literally held down by superglue and cannot move off the keys. Try playing *staccato* with each finger in turn. Play each note with the feeling of an upward (rather than a descending) motion. The sounds need to be as short as possible in the initial stages of this work-out, though it must be stressed that there are all kinds of *staccatos* in music, and the degree to which you can vary the length and sonority of *staccato* notes is vast and exciting. It should also be re-emphasised that *staccato* playing in particular can lead to physical tension, as the need for economy of movement can all too easily be corrupted by locking joints. Take regular three-minute breaks by dropping your arms to your sides, imagining that you are allowing your blood to circulate freely to your fingertips before carrying on the good work. Extend this basic exercise with separate-hand scale work, stopping before each hand position change to regroup all fingers over the next set of notes. Thus greater finger independence, wonderful economy of movement and a terrific sense of *leggiero* will evolve.

As the player develops the sensation of sounds seeming to rise on execution rather than being dropped by each finger, the sound emanating from the instrument will also become less ploddy, wooden and percussive. Speed can be built up to some extent by working in small units of two, three and four notes, but ultimately the close *staccato* technique in its purest state is not really very reliable as a performance tool. It is very useful for specific musical effects in performance, as well as for facilitating more technical control, however close *staccato* is fundamentally unsuitable for faster passagework. Use it for slower repertoire and experimentation in the practice studio.

Finger staccato

Next comes **finger** *staccato*, which is extremely effective in all kinds of scampering, effervescent, *leggiero* and *scherzando* passages (Bach suites, Mozartian runs, Scarlatti flourishes, Beethoven bagatelles, etc.).

There are three ways to articulate *staccato* exclusively from your fingers. The first form of finger *staccato* involves **direct depression** of the keys, the second is a **scratching**, backwards movement and the third is a **flicking**, forward stroke. In each case it is important to try to keep your hands as still as possible, letting your fingers do all the moving. Think of Irish dancers who move their legs but keep their torsos still![20] In a similar way, successful, coordinated finger-*staccato* technique manages to keep hands still (relate hands to Irish dancers' torsos) whilst fingers (equivalent to Irish dancers' legs) do all the hard work.

20   See the short film clip at https://www.youtube.com/watch?v=knSaCMcGSAI

Finger staccato work can begin away from the piano. Rest your lower arms and hands on a work surface with your fingers spread out comfortably in the five-finger position. Keeping everything still, try gently lifting your fingers up and down in turn. Only move the finger you are focusing on at any one given moment. This is not a challenging task, but awareness of what is involved will enable you to use the first, standard type of finger staccato, **direct depression** at the piano with relative ease in slower passages. Simply transfer what you are doing on your work surface to the piano, and you should immediately be able to execute finger staccato with direct depression.

Return to the work surface for the second, **scratch staccato** variety. This time strive for compact, coordinated scratch movements from each finger in turn. As previously, keep everything still except for the individual finger that is playing – in this case 'scratching' – at any particular time. When you can cope with one-finger scratches, try the technique in four-finger groups, beginning with your fifth finger and ending with your second. Scratch out the four-finger movement as quickly as you can so that it seems as though only one movement is involved. This should seem similar to skimming a pebble along the surface of water, or stacking up a pile of cards then gently nudging the first so that they all fall down. When you can scratch with coordination on your work surface, try the following exercise at the piano:

Presto

This exercise should be played both separately and together. It should feel like an effortless *glissando* movement with no involvement from the hands, wrists or arms. Eventually, when combined with the lateral movement described in Chapter 5, it will enable you to produce effortless scale runs at fast speeds all over the keyboard. Scratch finger staccato tends to sound much more beautiful than the name may imply. Indeed, scratch staccato is especially conducive to expressive contexts. The fact that your fingers are moving towards your body when you scratch seems to make the resulting tonal perspective less aggressive and warmer than is the case in direct finger staccato.

Flick staccato: the third type in the finger staccato list is the most brilliant and penetrating. It should be used for passages that require clarity, strong articulation and precision. Returning to your work surface, start preliminary work here by gently resting the tip of your left-hand index finger on each of your right-hand knuckles in turn. Your left-hand index finger should make you more aware of the pivotal role of your right-hand knuckles as you practise this technique with your right hand.

This is important: it is vital that no tension or effort is generated beyond the first two joints in each finger in flick staccato. You should feel as though you quite literally stop playing at your middle finger joints! In flick *staccato* your knuckles act as shock absorbers for the outward, upward movements that your finger 'flicks' or 'pings' away from your body and up into the air. Feel that the energy and momentum for movement is coming exclusively from the first and second joints of your fingers. Your knuckles must remain as still as possible. Imagine that they are paralyzed but keep them relaxed and comfortable in their immobile state! There should be neither strain nor stiffness in your wrist, and the hand should feel completely relaxed and still. When you have started to get each finger in the right hand working, try the same process for the left hand.

Thumbs will also benefit from the flick technique: flick the top joint of each thumb outwards with energy and vigour (this means a move to the right for the left thumb and a move to the left for the right thumb).

Practise each finger and thumb movement in this way: all ten of your digits should learn how to 'flick' and 'ping' effectively from their top joints. Imagine you are using your fingers like miniature catapults, or bows and arrows. Though this may feel ungainly and awkward at first, you should gradually gain in facility and the results after speed and control are in place are quite different from the other varieties of finger *staccato*.

Pianists as renowned as Mikhail Pletnev[21] seem to show an awareness of flick *staccato* in their approach to articulation in certain contexts. The touch is especially effective when you require clarity and energy in the sound, as is often the case in Baroque music. Experiment in practice by taking part of a Scarlatti sonata, or Bach movement such as this (Sinfonia from the C minor Partita). Try to retain relaxed coordination to match the clear articulation that should naturally arise from your flicked finger work:

You can practise passages with all three types of finger *staccato*. This will allow you to differentiate sounds more easily, giving you greater interpretive choice and also helping with your general technical development. In short, it will make you more coordinated.

21 Mikhail Pletnev plays 31 Scarlatti Sonatas. Virgin Classics CDVB 61961 DDD 2CDs

Wrist *staccato*

This approach can perhaps best be described as a *vibrato* technique. Using the wrist as a proverbial 'door-hinge', it is as though the finger is operated directly from the wrist (with the finger joints remaining fixed), swung upward, and then bounced downward to play. Obviously this is a percussive approach and can be very exciting.

A good example of wrist-*staccato* technique can be found in the opening bars of Rachmaninov's celebrated G minor Prelude Op.23 No.5. The repeated chords can cause inexperienced players to feel tired and uncomfortable. The technique becomes more comfortable and manageable if the rhythmic figure is tapped out on a work surface beforehand, with a feeling of 'rebound' or 'ricochet' in place for the first note in each repeated three-note chord. Try to feel that you are a seasoned percussionist when you work on this technique. Enjoy the sensation of articulating repetitions from the wrist. It is important to remain relaxed and feel as free as possible in both elbows and wrists as you practise:

In its most effective format, the 'back-swing' angle in wrist *staccato* is very slight and not really visible to the observer. Effortless velocity can be built up, leading to tremendous clarity of attack and virtuosity. Indeed the technique of wrist *staccato* involves rapid fire, concentrated ricochet movements from the wrist and is a pianistic counterpart to a string player's *spiccato* technique.

You can prepare for excellent wrist *staccato* by shaking your wrists in mid-air within a confined area. Imagine that you are literally shivering with cold let your hands shake freely but not too widely from loose wrists.[22] Next, transfer this technique to the lid of the piano or a worktop surface. Allow your wrists to vibrate but make sure that your elbow does not become locked in the process. Retaining freedom in your arms, neck and shoulders is vital for success and health in this technique. Indeed stiffness can make wrist *staccato* very challenging to say the least, and though loosening of the joints can prove challenging, progress will be possible when work is taken at a calm pace with a gradual build-up of both quantities of notes and velocity.

---

22   I am indebted to the teachers Susan Bettaney and Helen Krizos for this approach.

Reflexes and *staccato* emphasis from other anatomical places

For the sake of completeness, coordination and also for creative options which can be used in repertoire according to need and individual choice, I recommend exploring **elbow *staccato*** (where would the opening of Bartók's *Allegro Barbaro* be without this technique), and *staccato* from the **shoulder** and **stomach** (very helpful for the first entry in Shostakovich's B minor Piano Trio). However, I confess to viewing the latter two mainly as psychological tools for slower passages in my own performances. We may only play with our fingers, but we should never standardise the sounds we produce. As well as levering from the elbow, shoulders and back, pianists can visualise and place an emphasis on virtually every part of their body. With *staccato* I always prefer to begin with a strong emphasis on the fingers: this is always the starting point or default position.

Working at *staccato* techniques is extremely important for developing reflexes and dexterity. The flicking and scratching techniques outlined above under finger *staccato* naturally lead on to rapid-fire exercises for single fingers that develop suppleness, flexibility and controlled velocity. This is not only important for *staccato* playing, but also for octaves and general athletic facility. Appendix 3 (reflexes) gives a selection of rapid-fire exercises which naturally extend both finger-*staccato* and wrist-*vibrato* techniques shown in this chapter. They should be practised calmly in short, concentrated sessions. As with all exercises it is important to remain relaxed, work with sensible posture and to ensure that regular breaks are taken.

7 Touches: part 3

Legato, flexibility and rotary movement

> 'Flexibility is of vital necessity in healthy piano technique, and *legato* position shifts provide a natural induction into this subject, one of the most important areas for pianistic development.'

Much of our time at the keyboard is spent hiding and excusing the fact that we are grappling with a percussive instrument. When we try to 'sing' through our fingers, create a beautiful *cantabile* line, strive for richness of texture, *dolcissimo* sonorities and so forth, we are at a distinct disadvantage compared to string and wind instruments. Whereas violinists and oboists can honestly connect notes in one bow or breath respectively, pianists have to resort to an overlapping technique which by its very nature can never be as natural – as organically 'honest' – as *legato* from other instrumentalists.

Physical *legato*

Physical *legato* on the piano can be considered a 'faked' touch in the strictest sense, but the cultivation of effortless *legatissimo* is an essential skill for all executants of the instrument. It is impossible to imagine playing Chopin convincingly without the technical ability to seamlessly join groups of notes, like exquisite pearls in a necklace, into one enormous whole. In order to develop this technique, it is useful to practise simple scale patterns, hands separately at first, opting in turn for a slight overlap between each note, a moderate degree of overlap and finally an extraordinary overlap.

Set the metronome at crotchet = 60 then play a simple five-finger pattern: C-D-E-F-G-F-E-D-C with fingers 1-5 in the right hand. Though it is easy to play each note with each metronome (crotchet) tick, the challenge here involves holding the notes on *after* they've been played for specific durations throughout the exercises.

Try three exercises: set the metronome at crotchet = 60 and move up and down the five-finger pattern on each beat. As you do this, overlap in three different ways as shown. Firstly, play the pattern consistently holding each note for one-and-a-half crotchets (slight overlap). Then try holding each note on for a minim's duration (moderate overlap) and finally aim for a dotted minim's worth (hyper overlap) on each finger in turn:

Whilst it would be wrong to assume that performers consciously think of precise durations for which they hold notes on when adopting the 'physical *legato*' touch, exercises like these unquestionably help to develop a facility, greater coordination and more awareness of what is possible. In practice, the performer's ear will guide him towards precision with physical overlaps between notes. It has to be said that this is an extremely subtle art which varies within each phrase to a far greater extent than could ever be described in theory.

Finger substitutions

Along with overlapping exercises, students should cultivate the ability to effortlessly use silent finger substitutions on single notes. It is often essential to be skilful at this in order to sustain a *legato* line. One immediately thinks of fingering problems encountered in fugues from Bach's 'Well-Tempered Clavier' in this context. Whilst there is no substitute for experience, patience and extensive practice of examples from the literature, it would certainly do no harm to begin with scale patterns and attempt to silently change fingers once, twice or even three or four times on each note whilst maintaining a strictly consistent pulse throughout:

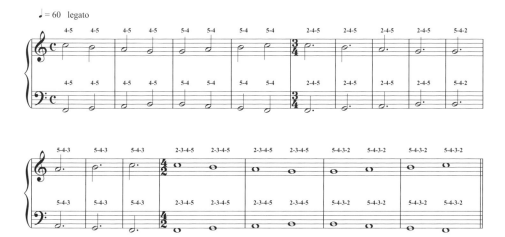

Finger pedalling

When physical *legato* becomes a feasible melodic, linear option, it is important to branch out and embrace possibilities in a harmonic context too. This is often referred to as 'finger pedalling' and is invaluable for creating the sort of texture which is sustained and rich, yet more focused and controllable than if the feet were solely responsible for connections. There is a whole range of overlaps to be explored, from the most subtle (ideal for Alberti bass figurations in the left hand of countless classical sonata movements) to the most extreme, as seems appropriate in the slow movement of Rachmaninov's D minor Concerto, or the D major Prelude from Op.23.

When your fingers start to fulfil functions which had previously been reserved for the right foot, the sustaining pedal is liberated and can be utilised in order to project even more tonal variety in the music. When this happens, pedalling becomes more creative, your right foot doing more than merely functioning as a bland, rather unsubtle '*legato* agent' that works whenever the going gets tough. Unquestionably this differentiation in use of the pedal is one of the main differences in approach between amateur and professional pianists. (Chapter 18 considers the right, sustaining pedal in detail.)

Legato overlaps

When it comes to interpretive uses, it would be wrong to limit physical *legato* to *cantabile* phrasing and finger pedalling. In a more general sense, *legato*'s skilful use can add depth, inner strength, cohesion and stylistic authority to countless scores. It is all too easy to play carelessly and with scant regard for finger connections. How often have we heard bad, non-*legato* student performances of the outer sections in Chopin's first scherzo? How often have pedagogues over the generations had to correct fledgling performances, pointing out that there should be overlapping connections throughout the mercurial passagework? The very worst pianism in the post-1945 era has often been marred by lack of *legato* overlaps, and skilful employment of the touch was indeed a hallmark of many a golden-age virtuoso. Even the flourishes of Liszt's first 'Mephisto Waltz' can sound much classier, more resonant and more authoritative when executed with consideration for *legato* technique.

On a more mundane level, practising with exaggerated physical overlaps and no pedal whatsoever is extremely beneficial if you need to feel in greater control mechanically. Work in this way will immediately improve security. I even go as far as to practise *staccato* and non-*legato* passages *legato* in order to feel more in command (as in the opening of Prokofiev's Sonata No.7, for example).

Of course it is also essential to be able to play smoothly *without* finger overlaps. I always warm-up by playing a slow descending C major one octave scale with no pedal in the right hand using only the fifth finger, the idea being that by relaxed coordination and depth of tone, each note in the sequence blends into the next. This is important because it reminds me to listen in between the notes and to try to blend the decay of reverb at the end of one note with the sound of attack at the beginning of the next (see Appendix 1 ex.8).

Pianists with small hands will in particular spend hours throughout their careers hiding the difficulties they encounter in not always being able to overlap notes. This is an enormous subject, as is discussion of all the contexts when physical *legato* is *undesirable*. Many artists strive for a more 'open', outgoing, bell-like sonority, and find as a result that conventional, overlapping *legato* pianism can seem too claustrophobic, drawing-room like and ultimately subversive. Though I personally would never go as far as the famous Russian (I prefer not to name him) who in recent times played the second subject of the Brahms' D minor Concerto with enormous hand movements off the keys on each chord (at times his movements were at least eighteen inches high!), there is no doubt that for special exceptions, deliberate non-*legato* movements away from the keyboard can have the effect of increasing reverberation from the instrument. In such cases it can seem as though the performer has literally learnt how to 'throw his voice' through the piano. This is especially true for 20th- and 21st-century repertoire. Such approaches may give many a conservative pedagogue apoplexy, but surely it is important never to remain fixated by theory when playing our instrument, and to progress by remaining curious and open to the unthinkable. Through embracing the unknown, creativity can continue to grow and ultimately flourish.

Legato changes of hand position

Learning how to move hand position whilst maintaining a *legato* touch can take considerable time and effort. Not only does it require pliability and freedom in the wrists, elbows and shoulders, it also needs firm finger work and economy of movement. The thumbing-under exercises in Chapter 4 make a good starting point for the mastery of *legato* movement across the keyboard if the principles of alignment from Chapter 2 are also borne in mind.

Chapters 9–11 will consider *legato* scales, arpeggios and broken chords specifically, but beforehand it is important to remember that all three areas of technique are entirely dependent on secure position shifts for success. Always focus on the thumb moves for security and control in extended passagework. Often it is one single thumb move that renders a whole passage insecure, yet students can waste time and energy by failing to notice where the 'thumb gremlin' resides. When fingering arpeggio and scale passages it is definitely most helpful to try and minimize the quantity of thumb shifts. Changing position inevitably makes the hand less stable and more prone to untidiness. Results will unquestionably be more successful and comfortable if your wrist is in perfect alignment with your lower arm every time you play with your thumb – don't be overly diffident when it comes to elbow flexibility swivel. Remember to feel freedom of movement as you shift from one group of notes to the next. Flexibility is of vital necessity in healthy piano technique, and *legato* position shifts provide a natural induction into this subject, one of the most important areas for pianistic development.

Flexibility

Behind firm fingertips and strong finger movements from the knuckles (the metacarpophalangeal joints) or 'bridge' of the hand, healthy and effective technical control and facility is largely dependent on freedom and flexibility of the wrists, elbows and shoulders. Experience has shown that students need to learn how to coordinate swivel and rotary movements in their playing in a more effective, concentrated manner so that hand-position shifts become more effortless, effective, graceful and pleasurable. Try beginning practice each day by depressing middle C with your right-hand index finger, holding the fingertip firmly down on the key, then swinging your arm as far as it can travel in all directions (upwards, downwards and from side to side). You should be able to do this with no sense of pain, awkwardness of inhibition. If you encounter problems, it is because you have stiffness. Flexibility will overcome this.

When developed over a significant period as part of daily technical regime, flexibility in the wrists can enable players with small hands to cope comfortably with stretches that they may previously have struggled with. Flexibility is important for pianists with large hands too. Indeed players of all sizes will feel more in control when they consciously study this often neglected area of technique.

It is all to do with swivelling, relaxing and pivoting from the fingertips, the elbow joints and the wrists. Pliability and freedom in these crucial areas will increase with practice and experimentation, leading to a transformed technique. I recommend pivoting on notes of the piano with each individual fingertip in turn. Take one at a time and literally swivel from side to side from your elbows. Your fingertips will swivel on the piano key surface in the shape of a smile. This is a useful basis on which to practise all swivel movements for stretched out intervals that require *legato* connections. Use a swivel fingertip technique on the first note in a large intervallic jump as a 'pivot' and it will be much easier to relax and reach for the second note you have to play. Flexibility unquestionably develops positively with practice and experience. Let's now look at some examples from the repertoire:

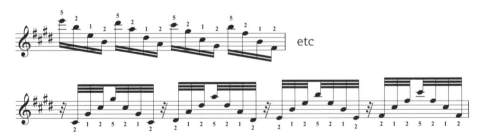

The opening two pages of Ravel's 'Jeux d'eau' are impossible to execute securely unless the pianist has the requisite flexibility and coordinated freedom for all of the right hand position changes. The example above shows some of my exercises, simple transposition variations, based on patterns from the piece. Transposition is a very effective method of working at changes of position, particularly if the pianist practises transposition with closed eyes.

This is part of a fugal episode in Bach's celebrated 'Chromatic Fantasia and Fugue' (bars 122–5). Bach's keyboard works are filled to capacity with flexibility challenges, and in this example my fingering is effective if you wish to play *legato* and evenly. It requires considerable practice and patience as the moves from fingers 1–5 and 3–5 will feel insecure and uncomfortable if you are stiff in the wrist or forearm.

Here we have the closing arpeggiated bars of Beethoven's Sonata Op.110 (bars 208–13):

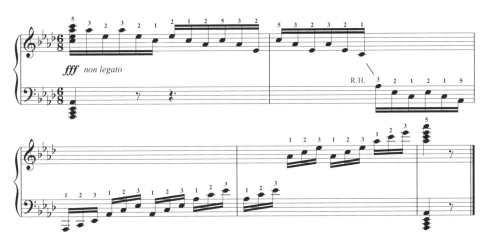

My fingering takes everything in the right hand in an attempt to synthesize the entire flourish into one heroically unified pianistic gesture. Many pianists would use two hands but if they do, they still have to try to make the passage sound as though it is being executed by one hand alone. It is worthwhile at least to try in practice to develop sufficient flexibility to cope with one hand in this instance, and even if a two-hand execution is finally chosen, the work undertaken with one hand alone will certainly improve your technical development overall.

Rotary movement

The controlled, relaxed oscillation of two or more notes or groups of notes is closely related to general flexibility and is commonly known as 'rotation' or 'rotary movement'. Whilst I would not go as far as some pedagogues do in seeing rotation as the answer to all stiffness and technical anxiety, there is certainly no doubt that it can free up many passages and provide a healthy way of overcoming both tiredness and technical anxiety. When mastered, rotation is an extremely pleasurable technique to utilise as it makes for far less effort. Tobias Matthay and his pupils were especially strong evangelists for rotation,[23] pointing out that music as demanding as Chopin's 'Black Keys' (Op.10 No.5) and 'Winter Wind' (Op.25 No.11) Études become much less onerous when practised with focused and relaxed rotary movement:

Rotation requires a sense of expansive freedom within a confined space as you rapidly swivel your lower arm and wrist in comfortable, oscillating movements that feel effortless. Begin practice away from the piano by simply cupping one wrist in your opposite hand. Relax and gently move your wrist from side to side, letting go and allowing your wrist to feel completely light and comfortable. Think of windscreen wipers moving smoothly from side to side and you will capture something of the movement required.

This approach should then be imitated by transferring the movement to the keyboard for simple two-note rotary exercises. Try these for fingers 4 and 5 or 3 and 4, with each hand separately, which Ronald Stevenson gave me many years ago:

Prestissimo

23 The renowned pianist, teacher and composer Tobias Matthay (1858–1945) wrote at length about piano technique. See especially 'The Art of touch in all its diversity: An analysis and synthesis of Pianoforte tone-production' (1903), Longmans, Green and Co. Also 'Relaxation studies in the Muscular Discriminations Required for Touch, Agility and Expression in Pianoforte Playing' (1908), Bosworth, London.

Once mastered, single-note rotation exercises should be extended into double-note work:

Accompaniment figurations can become much easier when realised with a sense of rotation. This can be seen in Alberti-bass patterns of all kinds, as well as in *tremolandos*:

Rotary movements can be found in all sorts of contexts. Pianists should be able to exploit them to the full, using rotation as a means toward greater freedom and flexibility. This will result in a healthier, more accurate and relaxed technical command.

8 Developing finger strength and brilliance

'Pianistic success comes from the requisite combination of finger firmness with total freedom in the wrists, arms, shoulders and neck.'

Finger strength

When Franz Liszt famously referred to Tausig's 'fingers of steel',[24] he meant that the celebrated pianist's articulation was able to rip through technical hurdles with phenomenal precision and penetration. Razor-sharp clarity, sureness of touch, supreme confidence and control all come from cultivating 'steely fingers'. At the end of the day, no matter how sophisticated, sensitive or visionary an interpretation may be, if it is executed with flabby, tepid or insecure technique it will remain an amateurish interpretation. You can be as poetic as a harp-playing angel in the first movement of Beethoven's G major Concerto, but without the finger-work to match your performance will inevitably fail.

How does one cultivate strong finger work? It could be argued, not without justification, that an awful lot depends on physical build and that those of sturdy disposition are at a decided initial advantage. One could also argue that a great deal of external, physical exercise, even menial labour (ploughing the fields, lifting bricks around the garden, working out in the gym, etc.) is extremely beneficial. Physical exercise of an intelligent kind must be considered positive for all kinds of reasons, not only for finger strength, but for the purposes here, exercises at the keyboard and approaches or attitudes towards pianism alone will be considered.

Just how much strength do you actually need to depress a piano key? Why can certain frail old ladies play with sparkling polish whilst many twenty-something students built like American baseball players only produce flabby, woolly Czerny studies? The answer has to be that coordination is actually more vital for good articulation than sheer brute force.

It must be stressed that finger strength does not imply stiffness. Of course it is vital to move fingers from the bridge of the hand: the knuckles (thumbs as we have seen are somewhat different). It is also vital to develop strong knuckle movements that avoid movements or 'collapses' in the first and second joints of each finger. I make no apology for re-emphasising the mantra from Chapter 1 about combining this strength with unblocked, relaxed wrists. Our wrists are our 'shock absorbers' and can be viewed as the proverbial pianist's gear box. Never allow them to become woodenly unyielding. Pianistic success comes

---

24 See Carl Tausig's short biography at www.everynote.com/piano.choose/0/103/19/0.note

from the requisite combination of finger firmness with total freedom in the wrists, arms, shoulders and neck.

Coordination

We have continuously seen in chapter after chapter that practising coordination can be achieved effectively away from the piano. If you want to stop collapsing the joints of your fingers and move each digit from the bridge of the hand automatically, then think about this concept constantly. 'Practise' whilst waiting for the bus, sitting watching television and just before going to sleep at night. You can also develop your finger technique by playing on work tops, your knees and closed piano lids! These approaches are arguably just as important as slow work on five-finger exercises at the instrument, which in this context should be done with care for the clarity of each individual sonority produced. When you are practising at the keyboard, make sure that you begin with simple finger lifting and dropping movements, without excessive height, but always with the most painstaking care with regard to control of each finger joint. Keep your hands, wrists and arms still, and focus completely on intensity and control of the particular finger you are developing at any one moment. In all contexts the player should guard against even the slightest finger twitch, bend or quiver: collapsing is completely out of the question, so aim for zero tolerance.

Injuries

Of course those with 'double joints' and past injuries may be at a disadvantage here, and will have to find their own way to technical control. Patience, common sense, perseverance and lateral thinking will certainly be required, and the aspirant should never give up hope. So long as one never induces pain or discomfort the risks of physical damage remain minimal. I also believe that if finger movement looks coordinated, elegant and controlled (in essence, aesthetically beautiful), then it is usually progressing along a sure-fire route to mastery.

Along with finger movement from the bridge of the hand, it is vital to 'grip' the keys as firmly as possible, as outlined back in Chapter 1. It is extremely useful to feel concentrated pressure on each fingertip in turn, squeezing that part of the finger, then letting go to allow each fingertip in turn to feel firm and independently 'taut'. Obviously it would be foolhardy and dangerous in the extreme to do this sort of thing without loose wrists and equally obviously, gripping each fingertip in turn should be practised away from the keyboard on worktops.

Gripping exercises

Once 'pressurised fingertips' have been felt and understood, it is useful to incorporate appropriate exercises into your daily warm-up routine.

Begin by 'bedding' D above middle C with your right-hand second finger. Making sure that all three joints of the finger are firm, squeeze the lowest (distal interphalangeal) joint with your left hand, then let go, but maintain a feeling of total firmness throughout your right-hand index finger from its very tip.

Next, 'bed down' E with your right-hand third finger, whilst continuing to hold down the D with complete security. Repeat the squeezing process for the E, then continue with F (fourth finger) and finally G (fifth finger) so that you end up with all four right-hand fingers firmly held down and gripped to the keyboard. You should then massage and rotate your right wrist using your left hand, with upward and downward movements, as well as in clockwise and anti-clockwise directions, making sure that freedom and looseness remains intact alongside the constant fingertip pressure and firmness.

Repeat this process for your left side, using your right wrist to manipulate firstly your four left-hand fingers (G, F, E, D below middle C fingered 2, 3, 4 and 5), then your left wrist in exactly the same way that you manipulated your right wrist. Finish off by repeating what you have just done in each hand separately, together. Play-grip the eight notes with both hands and maintain a sense of firmness and strength in every fingertip.

As well as checking wrists for stiffness, be vigilant over your elbows, shoulders and your neck. I cannot over-emphasise how vital these basic 'gripping' exercises are. They immediately expose any weaknesses in coordination management which students may be experiencing, focusing attention at once on an area of concern that can all too easily otherwise be overlooked. In sum, they encourage the essential foundations of technical mastery.

Articulation

So far, 'touch and press' weighted playing and rotary movement have been cited as the healthiest ways in which to produce beautiful sounds on the piano. High finger work has been viewed negatively, as a percussive, fundamentally tense approach to articulation that can all too easily lead to stiffness and injury. In defence of high finger movement, it has to be said that many students enjoy the physical thrill of building up powerhouse percussive pianism and of using the metronome to build up speed like a tread-mill. Students can also enjoy the exuberant, percussive brilliance of 'hitting' the keys and many young pianists do just that. The feeling remains that it increases tension and is actually less effective as a means of creating clarity than gripping firmly from the fingertips and moving firmly from the bridge of the hand.

As an example of razor-sharp, no-holds-barred articulation, the first movement of Beethoven's 'Waldstein' Sonata can be cited as a supreme example of a work that contains brilliant, blazing finger work:

Beethoven: *Sonata in C major Op. 53 'Waldstein' (1st movement bars 62–66)*

During a lesson, in order to illustrate a point, I once played part of Bach's D minor Prelude from book two to a pupil – firstly with high finger work throughout and secondly with prepared articulation (covering the keys before playing the note). Of course, prepared (or 'touch and press') articulation is vital for beautiful tonal production. I was therefore more than mildly disappointed when the young pianist in question said that of my two interpretations she definitely preferred the 'high finger' version! I think we have to respect this to an extent. We can warn students about the health risk, but if they are not using excessive tension and are practising sensibly, we would do well to let them get on with it. There are very few pianists who have not gone through a 'bash fest' period in their development. Pianists come in many shapes and sizes, and boys in particular can tend towards enjoyment of the physical rather than the aural in practice. Teachers should remember that reliable finger work ultimately depends on acute aural sensitivity, and this can be developed in many ways at different stages and not exclusively at the keyboard.

Rhythms

Certainly life becomes much simpler – too simple – if music is reduced to percussive brilliance alone. Closely attached to this hammer-and-tongs approach to pianism is work in isometric rhythms. The aim here is to bring greater clarity to passagework by changing the rhythmic emphasis systematically. Passages should also be practised in dotted quaver-semiquaver and semiquaver-dotted quaver patterns. Each of the four semiquavers within a crotchet beat is held in turn. The different rhythmic perspectives that result make the player give special emphasis to each held note. The grand total of six rhythmically altered versions of particular passages is to be practised in turn, culminating in a seventh performance which is played exactly as written. This is how work on the first two bars of Bach's C minor Prelude from book one of the 'Well-Tempered Clavier' BWV 847 would shape up if it were to be practised in different rhythms:[25]

25 As an alternative to the 'six isometric rhythms' try the 'four accents'. In a passage of continuous semiquavers, work in four ways: firstly accent and play *fortissimo* the first note in each beat, but keep the three other semiquavers *pianissimo*. Next, highlight the second semiquavers in each beat with big, *fortissimo* accents, keeping the first, third and fourth semiquavers in each beat *pianissimo*. Do the same for the third semiquaver and then the fourth. This method was suggested by the Macedonian pianist Simon Trpceski in a masterclass given at Chetham's School of Music in 2011.

Variation 1

Variation 2

Variation 3

Variation 4

Variation 5

Variation 6

Original version

Students can spend hundreds of hours practising repertoire in rhythms, and many teachers strongly approve of this method of working. However there are an equally large number of teachers who firmly disapprove of this approach. Are isometric rhythms a cul-de-sac or do they help build up your technique? To answer the question is to reach a crucial point in discussing finger strength.

There is nothing particularly wrong in developing the skill to alter rhythms in music freely. If a student finds it hard to play in isometric rhythms, then clearly rhythmic coordination needs to be improved. But how exactly do altered rhythms help your fingers to 'talk' more clearly? Over the years I have observed students practising in rhythms pointlessly, because they indulge in arm movement whilst they work. The central point about the fingers that is so often overlooked is that they function in a similar way to that of a stylus (or 'needle') on a gramophone. Bad finger work attached to a great musician is as sad as a faulty stylus attached to a wonderful hi-fi unit. The sounds that emerge from both will be bitterly disappointing. When working in rhythms, or indeed practising articulation in any number of other ways, I believe it is essential to begin by removing everything from the equation except finger movement. Think of finger movement as the motor within a machine, the essential mechanism that realises all the power and possibilities. It is so helpful to isolate articulation in this manner, limiting arm movement, keeping loose wrists and flexibility, powering intensity, concentration and power exclusively through the fingertips from focused knuckle movements.

Finger work

In the finale of his E minor Concerto, Chopin makes extreme demands on the pianist's fingers. Clearly high finger work would be stylistically appalling in this context, so work needs to begin carefully and slowly. Grip the keys firmly and use meticulously constructed *legato* physical overlapping between the notes. It would be wrong to omit shading:

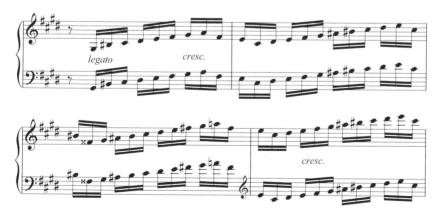

Chopin: *Concerto No. 1 in E minor (finale)*

What I am suggesting is that practice always has to be musically focused, right from the first stages. From this musical but 'finger exclusive' standpoint it is possible to argue the case for isometric rhythms. All methods of practising benefit enormously if they are interpretively engaged and technically focused from the knuckles with firm finger tips. That is not to dismiss arm weight at all, on the contrary it is to make arm (and indeed body) weight all the more effective when it is finally used. What is vital is that pianists can 'isolate' their fingers so that they can move them on their own with confidence and ease. They should work at scales and exercises from the 'fingers only' perspective, then add in weight as they choose. Provided work is undertaken with freedom and relaxation from the wrists upwards, healthy security will gradually emerge in their pianism. They will have the choice and facility to bring the forearms, upper arms, shoulders, lower back and then the whole body into their playing as they so desire. Of course, many would question this approach, simply because the human body is connected (for instance, when one thinks of upper-arm weight the wrist is involved, so why not describe it as wrist movement?). But the crucial point is emphasis. By becoming finger exclusive in practice in the first instance one immediately feels 'connected' to the instrument. To begin with arm weight alone is to feel more distant, to lose that closeness to the keyboard, and I believe it would be a mistake. (Of course there are exceptions to this, notably when dealing with students who have excessive stiffness or who are recovering from physical injury.)

Let's close this section with a word of warning, along with an exercise in prevention. The main musical danger of too obsessive an interest in steely articulation is surely that it can lead to an overly percussive, *martellato*, quasi-typist approach to pianism. Sure, there are special contexts in which such an approach is desirable, but if one thinks of the fingers as mere hammers, then the sound will become hollow, empty, ugly, lacking in personality and unpleasant. The notes will become isolated islands, leading to a lack of phrasing and to interpretations which seem too accented, literal and laboured. This danger is as serious in the Romantic virtuoso repertoire as in the Classical. One quickly feels a migraine developing when young pianists approach Rachmaninov's Third Concerto in terms of sledge-hammer articulation rather than in waves of colour, washes of sonority, torrents of liquid melody (fluid pianism does *not* immediately mean a lack of clarity). Equally, in Mozart it would be sacrilegious to opt for 'bullet-shot pianism' on each individual note when the composer specifically asked for passagework from his pupils which 'flowed like oil'. As an anti-*martellato* precaution, Phyllis Sellick used to suggest that pupils practise simple five-finger exercises with each hand separately on closed piano lids[26]. The aim should be to move each finger with appropriate firmness and strength, but to minimise extraneous surface noise as the lid is struck by each digit in turn. It is surprising how difficult students often find it to do this with a minimum of percussive sonority and clicks, but once mastered, 'lid exercises' can lead to a much warmer, less ugly tonal palette, with no compromise in terms of clarity and strength.

26   Lessons at Royal College of Music with Kathryn Page.

9 Scales

> 'Scale mastery leads to an awareness of which physical movements encourage velocity and which ones are more inhibitive.'

Some may consider it eccentric to wait until Chapter 9 before venturing into territory which most players immediately mention in connection with piano technique, but the reason for the delay is simple: scales in themselves are not central to technical understanding. Rather, they are tools which can be used to develop, enhance, illuminate and inspire (yes, scales can inspire!) healthy, dynamic progress. Every one of the previous chapters can be extended upon by the use of scales, and this is the basic point that so many miss. Scales are the vehicles in which you travel and certainly not the destination itself. Of course they are invaluable at the warm-up stage of practising, too. If you are tackling works in C sharp minor then it is very useful to play through a few scales in that key in unison, thirds and sixths beforehand. Scales certainly make excellent preparatory routines if approached quietly and slowly, with care given to healthy posture, relaxed practice, finger independence, economy of finger movement and natural, controlled position changes. Coordination can be built up by mixing touches between the hands, and of course the whole spectrum of dynamics should be utilised, not only to prevent boredom, but also to encourage in pupils the instinctive motivation to bring colour and tonal variety to their pianism.

A healthy dose of ABRSM or Trinity Guildhall standardised fingerings[27] will not do your sense of tonality, awareness of conventional fingering, sense of keyboard geometry, facility and confidence any harm. In fact, suspicion is bound to arise of any pianist who is not able to rattle off all major, minor (both harmonic and melodic forms) and chromatic scales in unison, contrary motion and with hands a third, tenth and sixth apart with ease. These are 'bread and butter' patterns which are second nature to any decent pianist, and it would be hard to begin any concerto from the Classical period without a firm grasp of them.

Basic scale practice

Scales can be enjoyable when approached in a 'music as sport' manner. A competitive way forward can easily be developed by using the metronome as the equivalent of a treadmill. Set the metronome at a slow speed (crotchet = 60) and start playing a scale with two notes to each tick. Once you can cope with the coordination necessary (no easy thing for novices as it requires rhythmic

---

27 'The Manual of Scales, Broken Chords and Arpeggios' (2001), ABRSM. Also Trinity Guildhall 'Piano Scales and Arpeggios Initial-Grade 5' (2006) and 'Piano Scales and Arpeggios' Grades 6-8 (2006).

awareness as well as the ability to focus on fingering, hand coordination and listening at the same time), increase the speed to 68, 76, 84 and so on. After about 112 you can go back to 60 but try to play four notes to each beat. You should find the sense of achievement very satisfying as you gradually manage to cope with faster and faster speeds. Inching your way up the metronome from crotchet = 60 to 180 (four notes to each metronomic tick) in every conventional *legato* scale is a very important process for any pianist to undergo.

Staccato and non-*legato* scales will inevitably have to be taken at least a little slower than those played *legato*, but attention should be paid to working at scales in all touches. In the initial stages of developing a holistic mechanical awareness and facility it probably is worthwhile recording optimum metronome speeds for scales with each touch, even with each pianistic approach. Once this has been achieved, there is a real understanding of healthy practice in place. Scale mastery leads to an awareness of which physical movements encourage velocity and which ones are more inhibitive.

Hand position

Mistakes in scales commonly occur at changes of hand position (i.e. when the thumb plays a note). It is important to work directly at the points where you change position in each scale. I recommend repeated playing of the two or three notes involved in each position change. It is important to feel freedom of movement as you change hand position, and vital that you observe how your arm and wrist moves as you play the notes. Do your arms and wrists enable your fingers to move over the keyboard more easily, or are they inhibiting your facility? Just how large (or small) does your wrist movement have to be in order to coordinate a graceful manoeuvre into a new hand position? Above all, do you feel a lightness and sense of physical ease as you negotiate a position change? If not, then you are not operating as effectively as you should be, and further study and consideration of your technical approach at the keyboard will be necessary in order to avoid injury.

With regard to scale coordination, the earlier chapters about separating finger movement from wrist movement, elbow and upper-arm movements and body weight, should be looked at again. There is no use whatsoever in belting out scales with loads of arm weight in the hope of developing finger strength. Far better to begin slowly, make sure that the hand is remaining relatively still, and then energise the individual digit that is performing rather than move the whole arm. Slow, thoughtful work can gradually be built up to a very rewarding extent. The scale patterns follow on nicely from basic five-finger exercises: building blocks of pianism that can be found not only in the Hanon and Beringer exercises already mentioned[28] but also in books of exercises by Tankard-Harrison[29], Schmitt[30] and many others.

28   Hanon Ibid, Beringer Ibid
29   Geoffrey Tankard and Eric Harrison 'Pianoforte Technique On An Hour A Day' (1960), Novello.
30   Aloys Schmitt 'Preparatory Exercises for the Piano' Op.16 (1922) Schimer's Library of Musical Classics volume 434.

Polyrhythmic scales

After conventional scale patterns in contrary and parallel motion are mastered, you can broaden your horizons. Do not forget that polyrhythmic scales can help your overall sense of rhythm as well as your pianistic coordination. You can practise scales in every key with duplets versus triplets, triplets versus quadruplets, and quadruplets versus quintuplets. These possibilities are shown in Appendix 2.

Formula pattern scales

Try also working on 'Russian' or 'formula pattern' scales. These can help improve your sense of confidence around the keyboard. Students often find them more entertaining than standard scales because they incorporate both contrary and similar motion work over a broad and varied range of the keyboard. I recommend the following truncated version of the 'Russian' Scale pattern at first. This is how it unfolds:

1 Play a conventional four-octave parallel-motion scale up and down.

2 Repeat the scale again but at the two-octave mark allow the left hand to descend whilst the right hand ascends two octaves. When this part of the exercise finishes your hands will be four octaves apart.

3 Without stopping, continue to ascend in the left hand and descend in the right until the hands are one octave apart.

4 Without stopping finish the exercise by descending with both hands in parallel motion for two octaves.

Here is a more extended version in G major. Try this after mastering the shorter version.

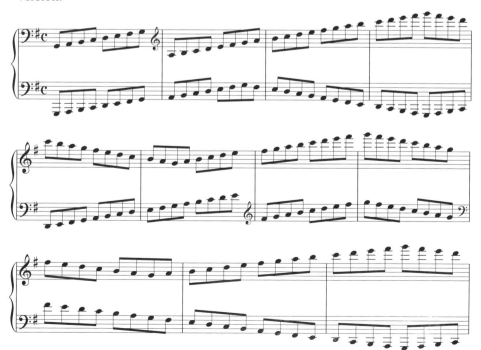

Of course this approach should be adopted for all major and harmonic minor scales. Eventually you should even be able to cope with the 'Russian approach' in melodic minor scales too.

Practice sequences

When extending scale work it is useful to have your very own 'scale sequence package'. This takes a single pitch centre at a time and can be rattled off in every conceivable permutation with no break, no hesitations, no unwanted accents and no stress. If you do take just one key a day and practise by playing chromatic, major, harmonic and melodic minor forms from that single pitch unit, you can concentrate your endeavours most effectively. Vary your pace, building up velocity for some patterns, but taking a more careful tempo for others (especially those near the beginning of the routine). In this manner it is possible to find fulfilling scale work in a session as short as ten minutes per day.

With the help of the pianist-teacher Norma Fisher,[31] I developed my own 'all in one' combination scale formula that incorporates scales in tenths, thirds and sixths into one continuous exercise after playing the scale in parallel motion. I find this extremely beneficial as it concentrates my efforts most effectively within one given key. Here is the formula in A harmonic minor:

---

31   Private lessons in Finchley, North London (1990).

10ths

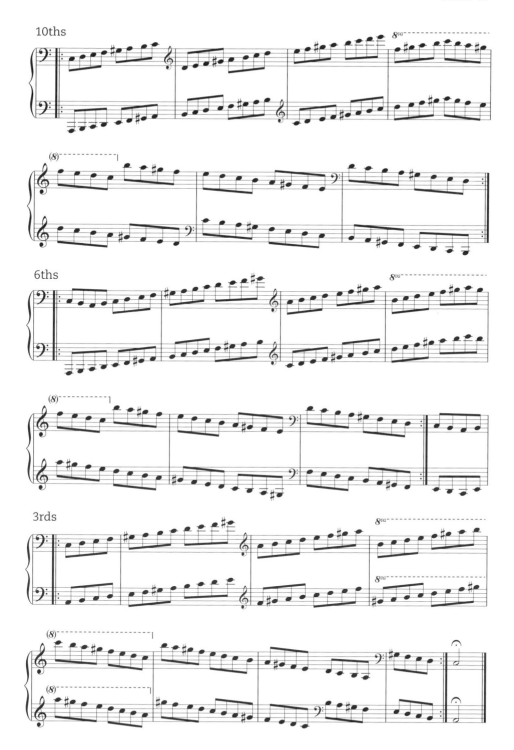

6ths

3rds

This is a wonderful way to build up stamina. You can set the metronome
going as you practise, taking four notes to each tick. Use the metronome like a
treadmill. Aim for target speeds and try to build up your velocity. Once you can
cope with *legato*, try to play additional repetitions of each part of the exercise
with different touches. This means that you play a four-octave scale pattern
in parallel motion *legato*, then immediately repeat it non-*legato*, then *staccato*

– with no break. Continue directly into a *legato* scale in tenths, then repeat it non-*legato* and then *staccato*, and so on. If you do this for just one key a day, you are working extremely hard and concentrating a lot of effort into a small space of time!

Vary the dynamics as you exercise, incorporating more than flat *pianos* or *fortes* into ascending and descending patterns. Gradual *crescendos* and *diminuendos* spread over each part of the exercise are helpful, whilst *subito pianos* or *fortes* added at random can keep you on your toes and they can also add a bit of fun to the whole thing too.

Scales need to reflect repertoire, so adding dynamics and varying articulation as you practise them is actually just common sense. If you practise scales in a monochrome manner then there is more likelihood that you will play repertoire in a monochrome way too, by default. It is much better to 'exercise' with colour as variety of sound should then seep into your subconscious, making your 'default' position immediately more musical and vibrant.

Fingering

The challenges of scales can also be extended by adjusting fingerings in unorthodox ways. If you can play all the major and minor scales accurately and fluently using only your thumb and index finger throughout, then you will be a master of position shifting. Alfred Cortot suggests this in the second chapter of his 'Rational Principles of Piano Technique'; he also recommends practising scales with different, limited groups of fingers. As examples of this, try playing a C major scale over four octaves in your right hand with the following fingerings:

1 and 2 alone

1, 2 and 3 along

1, 2, 3 and 4 alone.

Finally, try to play the scale over four octaves up and down using fingers 1-2-3-4-5 in strict succession throughout (5-4-3-2-1 in descent). For those with large hands and an insatiable desire for technical mastery, try playing four-octave scales and arpeggios in all keys, hands together, using only the thumbs and fifth fingers in succession. That is a sure-fire way to master flexibility and to coordinate position shifts.

Tone and colour

As mentioned at the beginning of this chapter, scales should be practised with a variety of dynamics and touches. Changes of colour and beauty of sound always make scale work vibrantly inspirational. There is a universe of possibilities out there which can be directly related to scale playing. What you choose to incorporate into scale work will depend on context, personal choice and your level. Teachers should be aware of extra-musical associations for scales, of relating them to colours, orchestral instruments, even to physical sensations and taste. How this is done will depend on the age, needs and level of the pianist they are guiding. As an example of inspiration via non-pianistic tactile association, what about playing a D flat major scale 'as though you are stroking velvet' or F sharp major with a sense of lemonade's (or champagne's!) effervescent sparkle and zest? Relating scales to music's essential connection with emotion and communication is a vital artistic necessity.

Scale work can continue to be varied and vibrant throughout your playing career if you explore patterns of notes away from the conventional major and minor patterns. Jazz pianists of course practise modal scales, and the revised ABRSM grade 8 syllabus requires candidates to play a whole-tone scale.[32] You can go further and practise not only pentatonic scales, but also octatonic scales (constructed by alternating semitones with tones). Ronald Stevenson goes even further by recommending that pianists explore scales based on Japanese pentatonic and Hindu raga patterns.[33] Scales should continue to be useful at the highest levels for all sorts of purposes, but most notably for sound production and tonal variety. As an example of how all-encompassing a scale experience can in theory be, it is worth remembering the occasion in Berlin when Ferruccio Busoni, on being persistently pestered to 'play' in an informal context (something which was anathema to his musical instincts), the great master eventually sat down at his keyboard and gave a visionary 'recital' of scales, apparently producing an awe-inspiring plethora of colours that surpassed anything those lucky enough to be present had ever heard before[34].

32 ABRSM Manual Ibid
33 Private conversations with Stevenson Ibid
34 Private conversations with Stevenson Ibid

10 Arpeggios

> 'It goes without saying that the more economy of finger movement and independence of finger work which the pianist can control here, the easier it will be to cultivate a truly economical technique.'

Non-*legato* and *staccato* arpeggios

As we have seen, non-*legato* and *staccato* arpeggio patterns rely on the pianist mastering lateral movement – the art of arm-wrist movement – whilst keeping the hands absolutely still.[35] Practise silently shifting the left and right hands in turn. Move the stationary hand up and down the keyboard by grasping the wrist with your other hand and using it as a lever for horizontal movement. It goes without saying that the more economy of finger movement and independence of finger work which the pianist can control here, the easier it will be to cultivate a truly economical technique. You should be able to play in this manner with arm weight, non-*legato* and *staccato* touches without the fingers leaving the keys. Shifts from one octave to the next should be accomplished with one single movement in which all of the fingers literally slide horizontally from the lower octave to the higher in a relaxed, quick, controlled and neat gesture. When this is 'up and running' it looks wonderfully poised, aesthetically beautiful and effortlessly professional. Be careful to avoid tension and stiffness in your elbows, upper arms and shoulders in particular.

It is highly beneficial to practise non-*legato* arpeggiation in blocked hand shapes with lateral movement and unconventional fingering. Try practising the above movements for all arpeggios with only the first and second fingers, then try with 1, 2 and 3, then 1, 2, 3 and 4, and finally, for those with 'tennis racket size' hands, try the non-*legato* fingering outlined in Busoni's mighty Klavierübung: 1-2-3-4-5. Basically, the longer you delay use of the thumb in scale or arpeggio technique, the more rapid your playing should become.

Legato arpeggios

We have already discussed the thumb and its use in Chapter 4. It is worth reiterating the need to fully master 'thumbing under' for *legato* position shifts before going any further. As the human body is symmetrical, it would seem easiest to practise contrary-motion position shifts for arpeggios before

---

35 In Chapter 16 we will see that in this respect non-*legato* arpeggios are remarkably similar to octaves.

graduating to the demands of similar-motion figurations. Thumb shifting seems simplified when both wrists are involved in sine wave or Loch Ness monster curves simultaneously, and the relaxed yet focused undulations of each hand will seem easier to coordinate when your torso becomes the 'axis' of all the shifting. Moreover, contrary-motion work makes it easier to analyse intellectually all of the physical movements involved, with experimentation a little clearer over such matters as how little leverage to use when lifting the wrists. Upward movements should be as small as possible, existing as they do solely to move from one position to the next. It is the lowest point of the wrist in its travels around the keyboard which actually coordinates with the fingers or thumb to play the notes.

All-in-one arpeggio patterns

Whilst many students find it useful to adopt the 'Russian Scale' pattern for arpeggio work, I prefer to do something a little different. This is my own personalized all-in-one arpeggio package which students have found useful for concentrated practice sessions over the years:

Root position major

1st inversion major

2nd inversion major

Root position minor

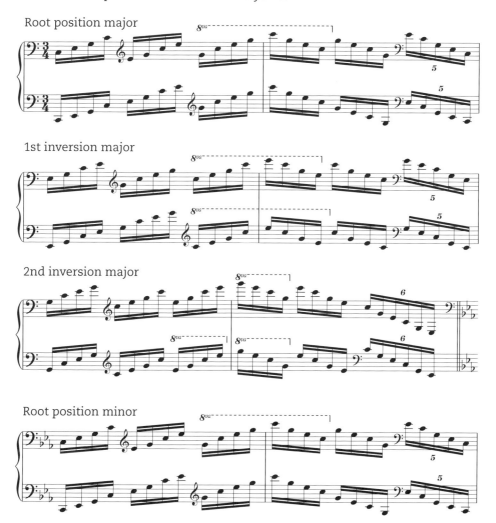

Diminished

Dominant 7th

Some practical tips for successful *legato* arpeggio playing

Playing arpeggios can be extremely frustrating and stressful for inexperienced players. As far as fingering goes, the standard solutions offered in most examination scale books (for example the ABRSM[36]) are perfectly sound and reliable. There is some controversy over whether the third or the fourth finger should be used on the second note of C major arpeggio in the left hand. In general I have found that students with smaller hands will find it easier to use the fourth whilst those with larger hands should be able to cope with either the third or the fourth fingers, and can make a choice based on the particular sound they hope to achieve in the musical context. Regarding 1st and 2nd inversions, it would seem appropriate to finger as for root-position arpeggios. (E.g. if the fingering 1-2-3-1 is used for C major root arpeggio, right hand, then it is simpler for the memory to finger the 1st inversion, beginning on E, 2-3-1-2 rather than 1-2-4-1.) This limits the number of fingerings that you need to memorise and also promotes flexibility as a suitable technical asset.

It is important to practise arpeggios in chordal blocks; C major two-octave arpeggio can then be reduced to two C major tonic triads. Play each triad, and then look at the real challenge of how to connect them. Too many teachers in the past have insisted that students do not move their elbows away from their sides when they play, and perhaps this is why arpeggios have proved to be so challenging for so many. The difficulty of connecting note three of an arpeggio to note four certainly involves considerable elbow movement, as well as careful coordination and relaxation. On note three your wrist will be parallel to the keyboard, but as soon as you begin moving to note four the elbow should swivel outwards so that when you begin to play note four your arm is at angle of 45° from the keyboard. You should immediately adjust the position of your arm, bringing your wrist back to a parallel position with the keys. This can all seem complicated and frustrating at first, so I recommend simply practising the move from note three to note four ascending on its own (as well as the move from note four to note three descending) until you feel completely comfortable and at ease with the amount of flexibility required. It is important not to use unnecessary elbow movement and as with most aspects of piano technique, physical comfort and common sense should be the bywords as you experiment and adjust in practice.

Legato arpeggios are challenging primarily because they offer precious little time to think about changes of hand position. For this reason it is a good idea to practise arpeggios by giving yourself *more* time to think. The example below expands the first note in C major arpeggio, allowing the player time to think in advance about the often dreaded hand move from note three (G with finger 3) to note four (C with the thumb).

Try practising this rhythmic expansion of C major arpeggio whilst singing or saying the words 'Tea, cup of tea' on a daily basis[37]. It should be worked at alongside the second example, which expands note three of the arpeggio, allowing time immediately before the change of position when the arpeggio is ascending:

Here the words 'Fish and chips' can help focus the mind on each repetition. You can also elongate the second note in each arpeggio and practise this third rhythmic variation whilst singing 'La-sag-ne, La-sag-ne, La-sag-ne':

---

37 I am indebted to Stephen Threlfall, Director of Music at Chetham's School of Music, for this advice.

All three arpeggio exercises should be practised hands together, and with your eyes firmly shut.

Don't forget the need to practise arpeggios with varying degrees of weight. There is no point in working arpeggios into blockbuster mode if you are about to perform a Mozart concerto! Arpeggios are similar to scales in that they require mastery at all dynamic levels, tempos, touches and colours. Impressionistic arpeggios will sound and feel physically more disembodied, 'floaty' and ethereal, whilst Brahmsian arpeggios have a regal resonance, a magisterial overview in which nothing appears hurried. Lisztian arpeggios (e.g. the final third of the celebrated Mephisto Waltz No.1) tend to 'spin' with excitement coming from the *quasi*-nervous energy generated from a very particular brilliance and finger-strong virtuosity. It is all a matter of stylistic know-how, priorities and the ability to adjust your technique to the needs of the composer. Perhaps the great 'arpeggio icon' prize has to go to the C major Chopin Etude, Op.10 No.1, a torrential tone poem requiring stamina, golden tone, vision and enormous strength mixed with velocity. Pianists need to be able to cope with the opening bars and the suggested right-hand fingerings (1-2-4-5-1-2-4-5). But let's end on a controversial note by remembering the de Pachmann fingering (2-1-2-4-2-1-2-4), surely directly inspired by Chopin's own assertion that the thumb was the centre of the hand and certainly an approach that eliminates thumb accents on weak parts of the beat along with a lot of stiffness.

11 Broken chords

> 'The technical skills learnt from practising broken chords in isolation apply to all sorts of other technical challenges in repertoire.'

It is my strong opinion that broken chords have had a raw deal in most technical manuals and books on pianism. Traditionally, much space and energy has been devoted to the necessities of scale and arpeggio work, but broken chords have tended to receive less time. In Oscar Beringer's celebrated 'Daily Technical Studies'[38] for instance, there are barely two pages on the subject, whereas 15 pages are concerned with arpeggios. Examination boards have often requested a prolific number of scales and arpeggios, but again have tended to pay little more than lip service to broken chords, with the ABRSM[39] terminating the subject at Grade 2. It is all rather mystifying as broken chords are essential figurations in Western music, and arguably their safe realization is more important in the successful performance of a Mozart concerto than arpeggios.

When they are practised it is vital to relax the wrists, aiming for undulating movements with the minimum of tension in the triplet figurations (for example, in C major this would be the notes C-E-G, E-G-C and G-C-E). Rotary movements are also commonly encountered in four-note broken-chord patterns (for example C-G-E-C, E-C-G-E), such as the one found in the first solo passage of Beethoven's C major Concerto.

Benefits of broken chords

Before applying this technique to repertoire, let's examine the benefits of broken chords in isolation. I would isolate three basic patterns of broken chords for practice, and recommend that each pattern be practised with each hand separately as well as together. It surely makes sense not only to practise these in every major and minor key, but also on every dominant seventh chord as well as using diminished-seventh patterns beginning on every pitch. This is what actually happens in most repertoire, and by equipping oneself technically in advance, facility and freedom is obviously gained for what remains the most important factor: interpreting the music.

---

38   Oscar Beringer Ibid
39   www.abrsm.org

Three patterns for broken chords

The three basic broken-chord patterns are as follows:

Pattern one triplets using fingers 1-3 (or 2)-5 in the right hand and 5-3 (or 2)-1 in the left hand.

Practise in all keys, hands separately and together.

C major (example)

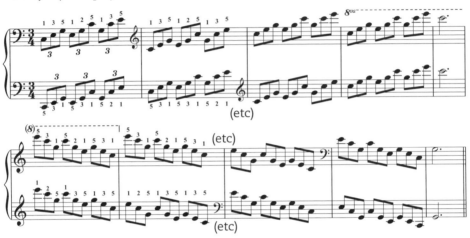

Pattern two chord shapes using fingers 1-2-3 (or 4)-5 in the right hand and 5-3 (or 4)-2-1 in the left hand.

G major (example)

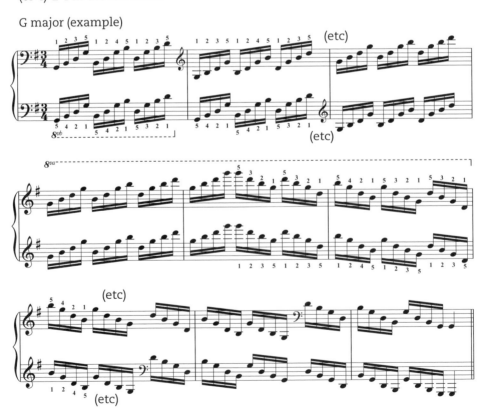

Pattern three rotary chord shapes using fingers 1-3 (or 4) 2-5 in the right hand and 5-2 3(or 4)-1 in the left hand.

A minor (example)

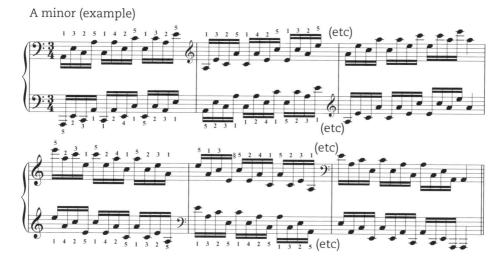

Pattern one

Care should be taken to move the thumb economically, gliding it over the keyboard smoothly and independently of the actual speed of the notes which are depressed. The wrists will gently undulate in mini sine-wave shapes, though attention should also be made to economy of finger movement, with minimum movement from digits which are not actually involved with playing a note. Ideally the third (or at times the second) and fifth fingers should move onto the notes they are about to play in advance, so that the player becomes conscious at rapid speeds of thinking only in terms of chord shapes rather than of individual notes. It goes without saying that elbows, wrists and thumb joints should be as relaxed and free as possible with broken chords, providing a foil for the concentrated efforts of the fingers.

Pattern two

The larger intervallic stretches will necessitate more pronounced sine-wave movements from the wrists. Unfortunately there is more of a danger of stiffness in this pattern, and more care needs to be taken with regard to the 'thumb-glide' aspect of execution.

Pattern three

This pattern is in a sense easier, as rotary movement of the wrist, when mastered, can greatly facilitate fluency and ease.

Obviously all of this amounts to a very large subject, but the technical skills learnt from practising broken chords in isolation applies to all sorts of other technical challenges in repertoire.

Silent practice

Clearly Mozart concertos are especially significant in this subject. With Mozart it is as though a proverbial spotless white table cloth is on display and the repertoire demands crystalline beauty of touch and effortless, co-ordinated control. Looking at the first movement of the great D minor Concerto, K.466, it quickly becomes evident that most of the development section is constructed from a sequence of broken-chord figures related to pattern two as outlined above. The late Eduard Weiss once remembered how he secretly watched Ferruccio Busoni 'silently' practising Mozart concertos in his Berlin flat, fingers evidently positioned perfectly over the notes on the keyboard as his hands glided from position to position, but without any sounds being produced[40]. Similarly, I cannot recommend strongly enough practising this passage in K.466 in this manner. Become a proverbial train guard, checking all 'passengers' (fingers) for misdemeanours and ensuring that the 'black sheep' of the hand, the thumb, remains suitably loose and co-ordinated. In fact you will quickly find that the success of broken-chord playing largely depends on the co-ordination of the thumb as it travels the length of the keyboard.

Slow practice

Broken chords can also be found in abundance throughout Beethoven's concertos, variations and sonatas. Practising pattern one can be inspiringly extended in F sharp and G minor as well as in diminished seventh sequences by approaching the penultimate page in the first movement of the 'Tempest Sonata' Op.31 No.2, just after the celebrated held pedal recitatives. Inevitably, more arm weight will be necessary in this 'heavier' repertoire. One cannot over-simplify the tonal variety of broken chords in Beethoven. The opening semiquaver flourishes in the first movement of the C major Concerto Op.15 require a degree of tonal sparkle and effervescence which is totally different to the massively regal pattern which features in the central development section of the opening movement of the E flat 'Emperor' Concerto. All of these passages are of immense value if practised slowly at first. Analyse the movements required as explained above. Decide on the amount of arm weight required and the tonal character of the passage. I also recommend that these passages are built-up by extending the length of the first note in a group of four semiquavers, then the second, third and fourth in turn. Giving yourself time to take stock on each part of the beat in turn is a tremendous way of accessing where you need to be at each moment of a passage.

It can be safely stated that the Classical repertoire exploits broken chords more than any other, though of course there are many examples in Scarlatti, and J.S. Bach's G major Prelude from Book One of 'The 48' comes to mind. Mendelssohn's uniquely fleet-fingered virtuosity also relies heavily on broken chords (the opening flourish of the finale of the G minor Concerto). Though

---

40   Edward Weiss, Busoni's last surviving piano student. From conversations with Ronald Stevenson. Ibid.

their mastery is less important in the twentieth century and virtuoso Romantic repertoire, the two-handed genre of broken-chord figurations reached unprecedented transcendental heights of breath-taking colour and display in many an Alkan score.

12 Ornaments

'Stylistic choices related to articulation can make or break technical success.'

Twiddles, twists and turns in pre-Beethovenian literature can cause all manner of frustrations for aspiring pianists, particularly for those with large hands. 'It is as though I'm walking on eggshells', 'I feel like a bull in a china shop', or quite simply 'I hate Mozart!'. These are some of the more common (and printable!) cries of anxiety I've heard over the years from pupils who have just failed (once again) to successfully navigate their way through a chain of apparently innocent, and intrinsically exquisite, lower mordents etc. How can such small, often lyrically charged species as acciaccaturas, turns, mordents, appoggiaturas and trills cause so much stress? There are normally several reasons for 'ornamentation angst': pianists tend to try too hard in a physical motoric sense, neglecting both economy and concentration of movement. They also tend at times of technical anxiety to 'switch off' aurally, becoming directionless in their approach musically, as well as becoming tense and stiff in their joints.

Ease of movement

The vital point is that in pre-Beethoven repertoire (and that for the most part means Scarlatti, Handel, Bach, Haydn and Mozart) it is essential to start from the assumption that everything happens from the bridge (knuckles) of the hand downwards. Imagine that your entire body stops with your knuckles. Keep wrists loose, but don't concentrate in the initial technical stages on anything other than firm finger articulation, working with independence of movement. Remember Chapter 3's principles. That means zero tolerance with regard to any movement whatsoever from fingers not actually involved in playing. Remember too Muzio Clementi, John Field and their whole school of economy (not that I would ever recommend experimentation by putting pennies or any other objects onto a student's hand whilst they play to you!).

Fingertips

Naturally mastery of ornamentation requires concentration on fingertips. Feel energy, focus and power in this area alone. Relax everywhere else. In approaching, for example, a Scarlatti mordent, trill or turn, begin with your digits resting silently on the keys to be played. Fingers not involved in the action should rest motionless on the keys surrounding the trill notes. Next, try moving only the digits involved in the trill, mordent or turn. 'Play' the ornament on the surface of the keys at a very slow tempo, but do not actually allow the notes to sound. Keep as still and motionless as possible, moving only one finger at a time, and keeping all movements economical, but vibrant.

Gradually speed up to the actual tempo required, but still refrain from actually allowing the notes to 'speak'. When this feels coordinated and comfortable, it is a simple step to go through the same process, only this time making sure that the notes are played out loud. Even for loud passages, it makes sense to build up from a soft dynamic, with *leggiero* and non-*legato* a very sensible starting point.

Period and style

Part of the difficulty with Baroque and early Classical ornamentation may lie in the myth that you need to be built like Hercules in order to have a reliable technique at the piano. We have already asked the rhetorical question in Chapter 7: 'Just how much strength does it actually take to depress a piano key?' The answer remains the same here as there: 'not so much!' If you try and bash the living daylights out of a Haydn trill, you will simply become tense, frustrated, make an ugly sound, produce pianism that is hopelessly unstylish and probably also play in a clumsy and unreliable manner. Another common difficulty with playing ornaments is stylistically charged: too many pianists assume that a spade is a spade with regard to pianism. Surely it makes sense to approach things differently in the 18th-century repertoire than in the romantic literature? Decorations and adornments in the Romantics must be approached in a totally different way from those in the Classical and Baroque periods. Style has a huge impact on technical application. The bias in Chopin, for example, is towards *legato*, yet the evidence shows quite clearly that 'physical *legato*', even in early Beethoven, was regarded as more of a specialist effect, with non-*legato* much more the norm. Ornamentation in Classical repertoire often flows more comfortably and sounds more crisply stylish when it is executed *without* overlapping *legato*. Indeed stylistic choices related to articulation can make or break technical success. This is a crucial point that is often overlooked.

Structuring ornamentation

Having separated ornaments into two crude divisions, it makes sense to go further and to say that *legato* ('Romantic') ornamentation can be less quantifiable than early Classical/Baroque ornamentation. Certainly it is very useful to develop the skills necessary to be able to play trills and know precisely how many notes each trill contains. In movements such as the opening in Beethoven's 'Appassionata' Sonata it is clearly of fundamental structural importance to a convincing interpretation that each trill is realised with exactly the same number of notes on each appearance. Below is a possible realisation of the opening trill in this sonata:

If you adopt this approach to this first trill in the work and strive for a classically unified interpretation, it makes sense to ensure that all the other related trills to this one in your performance are played with exactly the same number of notes. This can be considered a structurally cohesive approach to ornamentation and can easily be applied to many different styles of music. Conversely, the performer should have the confidence to 'let go' and play without awareness of how many notes he is trilling with. Developing this facility will enable you to execute ornaments that sound spontaneous, to be able to play as if improvising the trill, and to be able to do so without thought at different speeds, dynamics and with different degrees of weight. I am not saying that all trills before Beethoven have to be mathematically gauged, and that all after the great master should not be counted. As is so often the case, there are all kinds of contexts, and as an example of Romantic, 'free-spirited' ornamentation in the Baroque, I would cite the trills in Bach's 'Chromatic Fantasia' as a good example. It is infinitely preferable to be free here, adopting a spontaneous realisation of each trill that should vary every time you interpret it:

Single note trills certainly need to be practised away from the repertoire for security and fluency to be developed. For beautiful, even, 'Romantic' trills, try practising 4a and 4b from Appendix 1 as part of your warm-up routine:

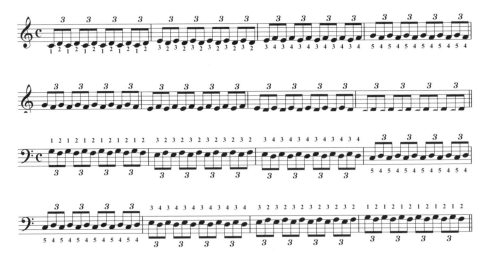

Performers all go through phases of claiming that they 'trill better' with one pair of fingers rather than another, and there is a school of thought that you should not trill with two successive fingers if you can avoid doing so (i.e. trill with 2 and 4 or 1 and 3 rather than with 2 and 3 or 1 and 2). However, it is surely sensible to try to trill as well as possible with every combination of fingers when you are practising. Space here forbids proper exploration of the possibilities of changing fingers for long trills, though many performers find this approach very useful, especially in the sort of trill which tends to occur towards the conclusion of Classical cadenzas in concertos. The following exercise exaggerates this tendency in order to explore possibilities and extend your technical facility fully:

Development of ornamentation within the Classical, 'economical' aesthetic can be cultivated by exploring the exercises at the end of the first chapter in Alfred Cortot's celebrated 'Rational Principles of Piano Technique'[41], but of course this is only a starting point: at all times it has to be remembered that ornaments adapt to the stylistic context. There are dozens of examples I could cite here, but for the most extreme contrasts think about the rotary movement mixed with arm weight required in the octave trills of Brahms' D minor Concerto (first movement), then contrast that with the delicate nuances in Debussy's étude 'Pour Les Agréments'. Look at the much more direct passagework in the central 'Night Music' section of the second movement of Bartók's Piano Concerto No.3, not to mention the encyclopaedic ranges of ornamentation in the thirty-two sonatas of the Beethoven and Liszt oeuvre.

41 Cortot: Ibid

13 Double thirds and other double notes

'... once the mastery of double-note playing has been achieved everything else will certainly feel much more manageable and comprehensible from a technical stand point.'

Ask any Russian pedagogue of standing which aspects of technique will improve a student's playing more than any other and the chances are he will answer 'double notes, double notes and more double notes'! The reason for this is quickly evident, as the successful realization of a passage in double thirds requires economy of movement, concentration of resources, finger independence, firm finger movements from the knuckles, loose wrists, an even tone, smooth, inaudible thumb shifts, the ability to 'voice' the top line in the chain of thirds louder than the bottom line (and vice versa), flexibility and the ability to 'divorce' finger movements from arm movements in one's mind. Quite a list, but once the mastery of double-note playing has been achieved everything else will certainly feel much more manageable and comprehensible from a technical standpoint.

The essential rules for double notes

There are seven essential principles which must be embraced for real authority in double-note playing. The first three: **(1) finger independence** combined with exact synchronization of finger movement, **(2) economy of movement** and **(3) firm fingertips** combined with total freedom and relaxation elsewhere, will hopefully be self-explanatory as we have covered these issues in earlier chapters. It is immensely helpful to think in terms of **(4) 'weightlessness'**, by totally 'letting go' in both arms, imagining that all that keeps each arm from collapsing downwards is a string, controlled overhead by a proverbial puppeteer hovering above as you play!

Fanciful though this may sound, if you have firm fingers and can really trust your arms to relieve themselves of stiffness, then double notes will appear remarkably simple, effortless, even pleasurable. Philosophically it will be as though they are 'playing themselves'. Whilst freshly energized and stimulated by this vaguely Buddhist approach I recommend embracing with positive confidence (rather than fearful dread) two of the most famous double-note challenges of them all – Schumann's Toccata and Liszt's 'Feux Follets'. Though I would never claim that all your problems will instantly be solved by adopting a lighter, more coordinated approach, it is true that things will become more manageable and give a more 'tactile pleasure' after this new way of thinking has been understood. Incidentally, all of this hyped-up terror that surrounds

Liszt's 'Feux Follets' boils down to about 23 bars or two pages of music (see the opening bars of this):

Even within those 23 bars there is repetition of material. Masterpiece though it unquestionably is, 'Feux Follets' nonetheless stands as an example of double-note 'hype' of the most discouraging ilk. With sensible practice the coordination challenges it presents can be overcome. Don't allow this étude's reputation and image to put you off – the collective fear that surrounds the piece is the result of a hundred plus years of negative, destructive pianistic hysteria!

The fifth principle for double notes, **(5) flexibility**, is particularly vital in the *legato* touch. Indeed, any succession of *legato* double seconds would be unplayable in a comfortable way without all the subtle, small wave-like movements, the different permutations in which the wrist travels from one note to another. Pivoting on one pitch to connect it seamlessly to the next is a skill which deserves to be practised until it does not need to be thought about consciously. Moreover, familiarity and experimentation over the years most certainly enables seasoned exponents to be more pliable and loose than younger, less experienced players (the reverse, in a sense, to the 'age factor' in sports!). The sixth principle, **(6) faking**, respects the fact that for at least part of the time it is simply not possible physically to overlap every note in a double-note passage (normally the lower notes). Finally we have **(7), slide fingering**.

With regard to (6), it is often vital to have a really strong, rock-solid grasp of the 'principle voice' (usually upper notes in double-note passages), with water-tight *legato* fingering, whilst the 'lesser voice' has to be cared for with special attention when the use of the thumb for two successive notes is required. Of course, pianists with smaller hands are more often required to 'fake' connections than those with larger spans, but for all players, ears are vital so that there is an awareness of bumps and unwanted accentuations. Lightness and nimble movements are requisite for everyone too, regardless of the 'stretch factor'. **Slide fingering** (7), is especially useful for fingering chromatic double notes. Sliding makes the impossible realisable, turning many an uneven, accented conundrum of a passage swiftly into lucid *legatissimo*. In general I prefer to adopt slides in the lower voice only in the right hand ascending and the left hand descending. Preferences are reversed for right hand descending and left hand ascending passages, which seem more manageable with slides in the upper voice. Experience has shown too that in scale runs it is easier to assimilate slide fingering into problematic contexts by only sliding twice if possible within the range of one octave. This normally means that slides are separated by fourth or fifth intervals. This can be clearly seen in chromatic double thirds, where the second finger plays F sharp to E sharp in a descending right-hand pattern, then slides from C sharp to B sharp. In the context of *legato* double fourths and seconds, increased usage of sliding may be necessary.

In addition to the principles outlined above, the importance of always approaching particular passages from a musician's standpoint cannot be overstated. So many challenges are made much harder simply because they are divorced from their interpretive *raison d'être*. This can be seen in the opening of Ravel's 'Ondine', where the difficulties commonly come from too heavy and forward an approach, with limited consideration given to the quality of sound desired for the atmosphere to be re-created. The Ravel example is also useful for the phenomenon of 'lateral thinking' which so often in technique can be based on new rhythmic approaches as a means towards successful coordination. When students begin to practise and 'think' the double notes in question as triplets rather than as groups of fours, much of the angst and stress disappears.

Double thirds

Begin by ensuring that fingering is absolutely clear for each third of the problem passage. It is vital that you can play both the top line and the bottom line of the passage on its own from memory. I find it particularly beneficial to ensure that I know the fingering of the bottom line for ascending passages in thirds, and the top line for descending passages. To help with fingering there are conventional approaches in numerous scale manuals and technical books (Alfred Cortot's 'Rational Principles of Technique', Chapter 4, is especially all-encompassing!). But for a wonderful immediate empowerment of technique, I strongly recommend that the so-called 'two-group' fingering be practised in every major and minor key.

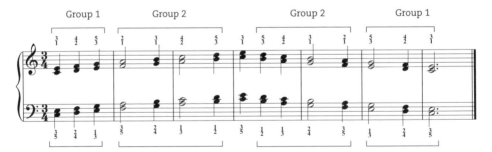

Start practising this non-*legato*, with the rhythm as shown, then try it evenly in straight crotchets (non-*legato*). Finally, try it in 'straight', even rhythm, *legatissimo*. Make sure that position changes are not corrupted by thumb accents. One of the major challenges is to try and hide the fact that notes immediately before changes of hand position in double-note scale passages have to be compromised, with lower notes in ascending passages playing for less than their full notational length, and upper notes in descending passages following suit. I recommend calm, quiet practice with the minimal amount of movement. It is vital to practise 'polyphonically', with firstly the top notes louder than the bottom, then the reverse. Students often find this difficult, but with patience, finger independence and suitable imaginative stimulation (think of infra-red beams shooting down your right arm into the particular finger), progress will be made.

Chromatic double thirds

There are many passages in chromatic double thirds, and this species needs special attention in practice before fluency can hope to be achieved in the great masterpieces. Personally. I prefer the so-called 'Chopin' or 'slide' fingering for chromatic double thirds:

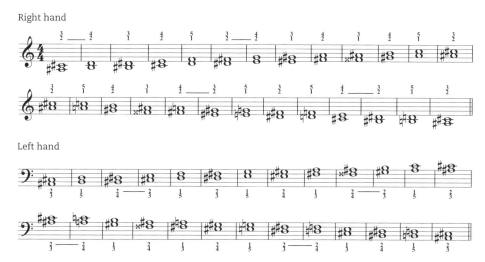

The given fingering requires the index finger to slip off black notes and once facility with this approach is achieved an even execution will result. It is vital to be able to play both top and bottom lines of chromatic thirds on their own, reproducing exactly the fingering in each case which will be adopted when the thirds are played together. As with ordinary thirds, the need for a perfect *legato* in at least one of the two parts is essential. The fingering given here will work successfully for passages in both major and minor thirds, and whichever note any passage begins on. It may take time to feel entirely comfortable, but once mastered, the 'slide' (or, as Busoni evidently called it, the 'sixth finger'[42]) approach becomes instinctive, like riding a proverbial bicycle. You certainly know if you can really control your fingering here by testing to see if it is possible to play chromatic thirds hands together, two octaves, beginning on each of the 12 pitches in turn – quite a challenge!

Many of the difficulties with double thirds in concert performance are psychological. Assuming that preliminary practice has successfully taken place, thirds should not really pose any more challenges than single notes. How interesting then to hear of rumours in which professional pianists became so anxious in the Grieg Piano Concerto that the Finale's double thirds were modified in performance as follows:

42 Private conversation with Ronald Stevenson Ibid

Original Grieg

Modified version

There is nothing especially wrong with this sort of 'rearrangement' in my opinion, provided the character and style of the music remain unaffected by the pianist's manoeuvring. If you 'cheat' and no one notices, then it isn't cheating. Those interested in this subject (and it can be fascinating and inspirational) should make a thorough study of Percy Grainger's edition of the Grieg Concerto (Schirmer[43]), which is not only a masterpiece in terms of reordering pianistic figurations, but also deeply provocative and revelatory in terms of pedalling and fingering. It also happens to be an important historical document.

One also hears woes and angst regarding the opening of Beethoven's C major Sonata, Op.2 No.3, with wild tales of use of the middle pedal and novel left-hand intervention by widely respected international concert artists (don't worry, I have no intention of 'naming and shaming'!):

As in the Grieg Concerto case, problems occur because of a lack of emphasis on the musical message combined with stress and a desire to try too hard in an animalistic or primeval sense. This all leads to complications, stress and frustration. The Grieg requires a 'lifting' approach musically, a feeling of taking the sound into flight. If one gets involved with accentuation, then disaster will inevitably ensue. Similarly the semiquaver thirds in the Beethoven example are all too often played more heavily than the longer chords which precede

43 Grieg: Concerto in A minor, Op.16, 2 Pianos, 4 Hands; Orchestral accompaniment edited and arranged for a second piano by Percy Grainger (Schirmer's Library of Musical Classics Vol. 1399).

them. They are often connected to the quavers that follow on, whereas in fact they are not joined to them – follow Beethoven's articulation markings which show them to be separated clearly. If these points are considered, along with the fact that the chords, semiquaver thirds and quaver thirds have independent colourings, then problems that appear can be seen correctly as more of a musical than a mechanical affair. The added bonus of this shift in emphasis is that practising will become so much more interesting as a result.

Of course creative fingering can often prove invaluable in double-note playing, especially when the shape of individual hands and, more importantly, the direction of the music are taken into account. Those with large hands who find conventional fingering awkward for the opening of Chopin's celebrated 'thirds' Étude, Op.25 No.6, could find the suggestion below useful:

In the early Classical and Baroque periods, problems with execution of double thirds can be resolved by careful voicing in favour of the upper line, awareness of the fact that shorter phrasing is often more musically convincing, and by experimenting with non-*legato* and *staccato* touches. This can be applied with success immediately to the thirds in many a Scarlatti sonata, for example Sonata in A major, K.24:

At the other end of the spectrum, in twentieth-century repertoire, the tone required is often more barbarically percussive, and the obsessive thirds that saturate movement one in Prokofiev's massive Sonata No.6 can be realised with appropriate fervour through arm movement. Try lifting the first third, separated by a rest, and then use three mini thrusting arm movements for the rest of the double-thirds opening motif and its subsequent offshoots.

Other double notes

Though double thirds are unquestionably more prevalent than other double notes in the literature, it is important not to neglect the others. It is vital that you are able to cope with 'mixed double-note passages', such as the magical filigree *pianissimo* section immediately before the central climax and cadenza in movement one of Saint-Saëns's Concerto No. 2. Also in the coda of the 'Emperor' Concerto's first movement:

Double sixths should be studied non-*legato* initially. Practise them in every major and minor key with lateral movement, keeping the wrist parallel to the keyboard and hand movement to a minimum when you are not changing position.

In *legato* double-sixths playing it is important to hide the fact that the lower voice in the right hand and the upper voice in the left are forced to use non-*legato* fingerings. Work at these two non-*legato* parts in isolation and try to reduce the detached quality of the sounds by listening carefully and emulating the approach suggested for the slow 'one-finger scales' in the warm-up exercises, Appendix 1. These depend on relaxation and coordination for success, as do double sixths. Slow and gentle moves between changes of position can work wonders here, especially if the 'legato-fingered' voices in each hand can be projected more strongly.

Those with very large hands may experiment with the following sophisticated fingering. Use what you can, then revert to healthy, comfortable non-*legato* when the fingering feels uncomfortable or simply not practical. If you omit all the finger substitutions then this fingering is also useful for every major and minor *staccato* scale in double sixths. But when using the fingering for *legato* purposes, lots of elbow flexibility will enable you to keep your wrist and lower arm in alignment, so preventing injury. This is important as the fingering is especially extreme: it is designed for maximum overlaps between notes and so leads on to the other 'slide' fingerings for more unusual double-note scales:

Here are some rarer birds which need to be considered by those interested in contemporary repertoire, as well as by pianists who wish to have a truly exhaustive, 'Faustian' technique ready for any eventuality.

Double major seconds (successions of these immediately sound mystical and celestial, and are excellent not only for stimulating improvisatory skills but also for coming to grips with 'slide' fingering):

Double fourths and fifths are even more unusual, though they can occur in the standard repertoire as part of a flourish at the end of a section, often with the left hand playing single notes so a succession of brilliant chromatic triads results:

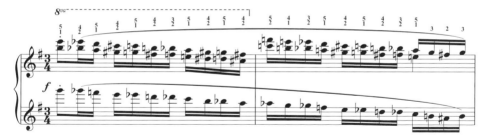

Like double sixths, fingering for double fourths and double fifths will depend on how large your hand is. Inevitably there are also lots of personal preferences that will vary from pianist to pianist with fingering, but here are my own solutions. Do remember that I have a large hand, favour slide fingering and try to make every connection as 'overlapped' as possible between notes. If you have a small hand, then the following will probably not work for you. Please do not use these fingerings if they cause any strain, pain or discomfort whatsoever:

Double fifths as first-inversion chords in sequences:

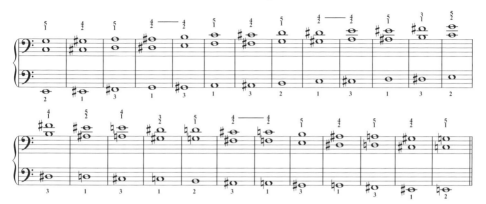

Finally we can even consider **double sevenths**. Try experimenting with *legato* work in Ronald Stevenson's extraordinary 'Fugue on a fragment of Chopin' (1949), a piece which springboards towards the unknown from traditional *legato* double-note technique:

Seven principles for double note playing:

(a) Finger independence and synchronization

(b) Economy of movement

(c) Firm finger-tips combined with freedom

(d) Weightlessness: 'Letting go'

(e) Flexibility

(f) 'Faking' overlaps in one voice

(g) Slide fingering

14 Repeated notes

'Imagine you are tickling the keys, allowing the notes to speak at the very threshold of sound…'

Passages involving the rapid repetition of individual notes can be among the most frustrating moments in performance. Students frequently complain of 'seizing-up' when attempting to execute repeated notes. How sad that these technical effects so often fail to function convincingly in practice, for when executed with authority, repeated-note figurations offer a tremendous breadth of opportunity. It is not simply that they are mesmerizing and colourful in themselves; the successful articulation of repeated-note passages demands an effortless coordination and degree of control that will benefit all other aspects of piano technique. A lack of know-how in the execution of repeated notes can lead to groups of notes failing to 'speak' at all. Even worse, the physical and psychological tension resulting from a mental block can lead to long-term anxiety about the 'repetition problem' throughout the repertoire. This tension impacts on other aspects of playing, resulting in a downward technical spiral and depressing consequences all round. However, with a little thought and practice, repeated notes can be mastered and even enjoyed.

Repeated notes in theory

Firstly, don't blame your piano. While the action may not be functioning perfectly, learn to accept graciously that it is not always possible to drive an upright at the same speed as a Model D Steinway. Find a comfortable pace at which the instrument can articulate repetition and respect it. On one infamous occasion during the semi-finals of the Leeds International Piano Competition many years ago, questions were raised about the quality of the action on the chosen instrument. A group of the semi-finalists in the competition opted to play that *tour-de-force* of repetitive action, Ravel's 'Scarbo', and the BBC broadcast extracts of repeated notes from this movement played by each pianist in turn, highlighting the challenges faced in navigating through uncomfortable terrain. The impression left was that if pianists as skilful as Leeds semi-finalists find it hard to cope with repeated notes on a concert instrument, there cannot be much hope for less advanced players on domestic instruments. Let's try and be a little more positive than that and find ways in which the technique can be approached positively by everyone.

Firstly, do try out the exercises to be played by single fingers in Appendix 3: Reflexes (referred to originally in Chapter 6, *Staccato*). This will encourage velocity and control. But we are now concerned with using more than one finger to articulate rapid and clear definition when playing repeated notes. Begin working with two-note 'rebound' repeated-note exercises, playing a note with the third finger, then allowing the key as it rebounds to touch your second

finger as your finger drops downward. Played properly, the second finger plays
the note by default, with no effort whatsoever.

Rebound exercises

Practise rebound exercises hands separately, then together, in all the
combinations of two-note fingerings (3-2, 2-3, 4-3, 3-4, 4-5, 5-4, 2-1, 1-2). Next,
try three-note rebound exercises, beginning with fingerings 4-3-2, 2-3-4, 3-2-1
and 1-2-3, hands separately and then together. For more of a challenge, try 5-4-
3 and 3-4-5. Finally try combinations that use all four fingers at a time.

Practise hands separately and together: 2-note patterns

3-note patterns

More challenging

All four fingers in each hand

In all repeated-note work it is essential to feel loose, with a sensation of weightlessness. Imagine that the bridge of each hand is the only area requiring effort, and that everything else is free. Forget about playing 'deeply' and making the keys go down to the proverbial 'bed' of the keyboard (something we will return to later). It is more helpful to think lightly and try to depress the keys as sparingly as possible. Work on the surface. This is the crucial thing to remember and it determines clarity in repetition more than anything else. It is far harder to play repetitive notes with a heavy, 'deep-bedded' touch than with a *leggiero* approach. Imagine you are tickling the keys, allowing the notes to speak at the very threshold of sound before going for a rebound action with your next finger.

It is important to continue practising repeated notes in extended sequences via the use of circular movement. Observe your elbows and concentrate on clockwise or anti-clockwise movements as patterns of triplets repeated on single notes. Enjoy the sensation of 'letting go' and allow logical finger patterns to emerge. A useful tip is to sing every repeated-note figuration out loud; vocalising can make the challenge so much easier.

Repetitions in the repertoire

The following illustrate the principles outlined above. The opening of the development section of the first movement of Prokofiev's Violin Sonata No.2 illustrates 'rebound repetitions' very nicely and is certainly worth practising for hands-together coordination.

The repeated notes in Liszt's 2nd Hungarian Rhapsody need to be worked at lightly and with a 'rebounding' finger articulation.

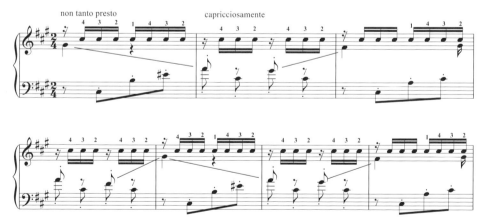

From the solo repertoire and for left-hand repeated notes, Busoni's 'Turandots Frauengmach' (Elegy No.4) is a direct extension of the outlined rebound exercises.

For extended sequences using an easily remembered fingering, try the most infamous repeated-note challenge of them all, Ravel's 'Alborada del Gracioso' (below). This notorious graveyard becomes so much easier when vocalization, weightlessness, playing on the surface of the keys and rotary techniques are adopted. My suggested fingering makes for a neater, clearer overall approach than is sometimes the case. In time it should be possible to execute this particular number with complete confidence and élan.

15 Chords

> 'Always prepare a chord in advance by shadowing the notes immediately before playing them.'

As the piano is essentially a harmonic instrument, playing chords should feel natural and effortless. A relaxed facility in this area of technique is essential for much of the repertoire, yet progress is often hampered by stiffness and a lack of confidence, dexterity and velocity. Chordal sequences are often beset by further problems, including inefficient fingering, clumsy accents, physical exhaustion, a lack of power and limited tonal variety. 'Chordal angst' often translates as 'tonal angst' for the audience, with the pianist's technical stress resulting in a less-than-beautiful sound. Pianists with small hands may panic when faced with chords with a wide spread of notes, and even those blessed with *quasi*-Rachmaninov spans may not be able to see the wood for the trees in densely textured chordal passages. But there are solutions to all these issues.

Shadowing

Playing chords successfully starts with a relaxed arm-weight. Begin by playing an ascending and descending C major chord sequence in three parts, then four parts, hands separately and together:

Always prepare a chord in advance by 'shadowing' the notes immediately before playing them. This split-second preparation will radically improve the sound quality and accuracy of the chord and give a sense of space and calmness to your playing. Elbow joints, wrists and shoulders should remain relaxed, fingertips firm on the keyboard and arm movement coordinated. Percussive chordal textures, where the quick-fire execution of parallel chords requires loose, strong wrists will also benefit from this initial approach. Experienced performers may choose to begin off the keys rather than from the 'touch and press' position, in order to create more 'attack' and energy.

Large chords

With chords that are 'impossible' to reach, remember the laws of acoustical theory and harmonic partials: if you must miss out a note or two, ensure that some of the remaining notes include the missing note(s) in their sequence of harmonics. The trick is to balance the 'doctored' chord so that your tracks are hidden. The great Spanish pianist Alicia de Larrocha, who had a small stretch, has given many memorable performances of works containing titanic chordal passages.[44]

Finger substitution

Melodic phrases which are really a sequence of chords can prove challenging: the pianist must connect the top notes of each chord into a beautiful, seamless and accent-free phrase, while remaining truthful to the lower notes. Bringing out that top melody requires silent finger changes similar to those used by organists (finger substitution). By combining finger substitution for the melody with the quick release of the notes underneath, fluency can be achieved. This technique is necessary if you wish to play the second subject from Brahms' Piano Concerto No.1 with conviction:

Tonal balancing

Flexible wrists and elbows, with deft pedalling and tonal balancing, will add further polish. Similarly, the musical context of a chord can be dramatically altered by projecting a different note within it. Try repeating four- and five-part chords in isolation, bringing out a different note each time, without any tension or stiffness. I strongly recommend using the extraordinarily beautiful opening of Beethoven's Piano Concerto No.4 as a creative daily exercise to develop this approach as it contains five, six and eight-note chords which have the potential to be as magical as anything in the entire repertoire when performed by a great artist. After all, if you are working seriously and regularly at your technique, why not ensure that your daily bread is of the very highest quality!

44 Alicia de Larrocha plays Rachmaninov Piano Concerto No. 3 in D minor on YouTube: www.youtube.com/watch?v=UTraM4cQ.

Generally speaking, it is not advisable to think separately in terms of the technical and interpretative challenges of chords. Mechanical realisation has to go hand in hand with musical intention. The opening of Bach's Prelude in B flat minor ('The Well-Tempered Clavier' Book 1) is an example of this, as is the opening theme in the first movement of Mozart's Sonata in A, K.331 and the entire second movement of Beethoven's Sonata in G, Op.14 No.2. In these cases the performer's ear must be acutely aware of balancing and tonal hierarchies. Listen and listen again. 'Musical' playing is mainly playing that takes balancing between the textures into consideration. Indeed tonal balancing in chordal playing provides us with a multitude of possibilities.

In the Romantic repertoire there are scores of passages where the balancing of chords can transform results. Projecting one voice over another can make a familiar passage sound totally unfamiliar. Try this out in Chopin's Prelude in C minor and the opening of Rachmaninov's Piano Concerto No.2. These two are particularly good sonority tests for both instruments and players. See how many different ways you can re-interpret the example below (Rachmaninov's final Prelude Op.32 No.13). Experimenting in this way will give you hours upon hours of limitless pleasure and discovery. The re-voicing and re-balancing of a tonal hierarchy is unquestionably one of the most pleasurable aspects in all of piano technique. Explore, re-define and enjoy!

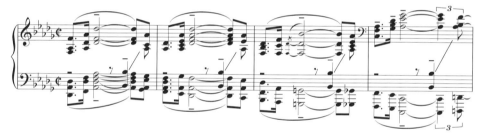

Percussive chords

For rapid-fire percussive chords that require flexible yet steely wrists, look no further than the 'Danse Russe' transcription by Stravinsky from 'Petrushka'. This requires firm focus in the fingertips and rapid quick-fire wrist movement.

Chordal washes

At times in the repertoire a series of chords needs to be blended into a glorious tonal arch of golden sonority. With a confident, relaxed arm movement and generous use of the sustaining pedal, the pianist can 'lift' a chord out of the piano, listen to the ensuing resonance as it floats around the room, then feel that sonority flow through the arms into the next chord. A veritable tonal loop is thus created as the process repeats itself, building up the decibel level in the most beautiful way.

Floating chords and tonal loops abound in Debussy's 'La cathédrale engloutie', but our final example here, the opening of Tchaikovsky's Piano Concerto No.1,

allies these qualities to a truly golden tonal range. These are chords which
(when approached with suitable élan, weight from the full body and energy)
can truly lift the spirit.

16 Octaves

> **'It is important to recognise that certain octave runs need to be deeper and richer than others and that the whole gamut of colour and touch needs to be adopted in octave playing – just as in every other type of pianism.'**

Octaves have a glitzy, glamorous image similar to the so-called 'smash' in lawn tennis. Both can be spectacular, extremely exciting and impressive, especially at climaxes and key moments. It is true to say that neither, if approached with intelligence, coordination and understanding, are especially difficult. Octaves can be awkward for those with small hands, but provided the requisite span can be reached without undue effort there is no reason for fluency and comfort not to be within reachable grasp after practice and consideration.

Single-note scales

Begin with single-note scales played by the fifth finger in each hand alone. Practise slowly at first, building up the comfort factor until you feel well co-ordinated. It is important to feel completely at ease with the mini-undulations from the wrist which are necessary for effective movement between each octave. Be careful over your wrist-arm alignment, as outlined back in Chapter 2. To a large extent it's the degree to which looseness and flexibility can be achieved in the wrist which will ultimately determine how rapid and accurate your fifth-finger scales will be. It is good to extend this practice by trying to play scale patterns with both fifth fingers two octaves apart, then to try fifth-finger work with arpeggios:

Octave scale patterns

Move on to actual octave practice itself, but only with slow, quiet practice at first, using scale patterns. Keep the emphasis on movement from the wrist and arm rather than from the hand: one of the most common problems with octaves arises from the belief that the hand should 'lead' the arm, moving forward ahead of the rest of the limb. Actually it is vital to feel a sensation of undulating yet economical, coordinated movement across the keyboard, coming from the wrist, the forearm or the upper arm (or indeed even from the shoulder, the upper torso or the whole body in certain circumstances). Remember the principles of lateral movement and alignment and you won't go far wrong.

Metronome practice

Part of the gradual developmental training for octaves should involve octave scale and arpeggio metronome practice. Set the machine at crotchet = 60 and try four notes to each metronome tick, before beginning to inch up towards a more virtuosic tempo (crotchet = 63 after a week, then 66, 69, 72 and so on). Obviously it is vital not to strain, and mini-breaks of even a few seconds every five minutes are vital for health and well-being. As in other branches of technique, it is useful to practise without staring at either your hands or the keyboard. 'Blind practice' is a sure means of building control.

Variety of approach

It is simply too restrictive for an interpreter who wishes to have many options in performances to approach octaves in only one way. Obviously it is important to recognise that certain octave runs need to be deeper and richer than others and that the whole gamut of colour and touch needs to be adopted in octave playing just as in every other type of pianism. Let's continue with some contrasted examples of octaves from the repertoire to give a flavour of the variety of approach necessary for authority in performance.

The central section of Chopin's 'Heroic' Polonaise in A flat Op.53 contains one of the most celebrated left-hand octave 'stunts' in pianistic literature:

The gradual build-up of sonority as a four-note descending semiquaver scale fragment in E major is relentlessly reiterated and is frequently cited by amateur players as an example of a passage where tiredness can defeat them, even to the extent that the whole left side seems to seize up. The passage implies rotary movement in an anti-clockwise direction and when priority is given to the B as a leading note and the E as 'star note' (requiring more emphasis) then the passage flows more easily. In any case, the movements here can be thought of as from the wrist, with minimum involvement from the upper arm.

Economy and concentration of movement from the wrist is also helpful when dealing with the right-hand repeated-note octaves in the closing section of Liszt's 'La Campanella' and towards the end of the development in Schumann's 'Toccata'. Without suitable consideration being given to freedom and looseness in the elbow and upper arm in these 'hot spots', proper mastery is going to be challenging, to say the least:

But what of the real 'block-buster' octave challenges? Let's take a look at the first concertos of Tchaikovsky and Liszt, arguably the two most celebrated examples in this context. The final pre-coda octave flourish in the third movement of the Tchaikovsky always brings a mass mock-heroic gasp of air from orchestral players in rehearsal, and needs to be executed as though the thousands of notes are played in one massive, continuous movement. The secrets of success come from extended practice of the thumbs alone, as well as the feeling that it is always a horizontal technical challenge in the passage, rather than a vertical 'down-up-down-up' one. The pianist has to be able to 'let go' completely, to 'spin' with exuberant abandon and élan. Inevitably the wrists will appear raised rather more than they would in single-note playing, and inevitably the player will feel a sensation of losing himself to the extent that it is as if the octaves are playing themselves.

In the Liszt Concerto in E flat it is difficult to find a single page where octaves are not present. But no section in the piece is as well discussed as the very opening, containing potentially treacherous leaps from a dominant pedal springboard. Again, there should not be any problem here if sufficient emphasis is given in preparation to horizontal movement, following the line, remaining close to the keys, and coordinating firmness with freedom in the appropriate anatomical places:

Space forbids more than passing reference to some of the other 'octave types' frequently encountered. Much of the brittle, percussive sound found in contemporary octave writing (Bartók's 'Allegro Barbaro' and so on) is effectively realised from the elbows, though Debussy's 'Pour Les Octaves' Étude requires more *cantabile*, finesse and variety of tone. Brahms demands resonance and richness in super-abundance; full arm weight at the beginning of the development in the opening movement of the Concerto in D minor should not be confused with the approach necessary in the Liszt and Tchaikovsky concertos. On the other hand, the 'water-tight' overlapping finger work necessary in variation six of the Brahms Handel Variations is different yet again, as is the moderately sonorous approach recommended for the remarkable octaves in the first movement of Beethoven's Sonata in F major, Op.54:

Finally, consideration should be given to acquiring a fluent 'glissandi-octave'
technique, necessary for the third movement of Stravinsky's 'Petrushka'
transcription, as well as Variation 13 in Book One of the Brahms Paganini
Variations. Heavy finger work is anathema to success here. In order to make the
octaves flow you have to use as shallow a touch for articulation as possible.

It is also extremely useful to focus on the thumb notes rather than the fifth-
finger notes. If you can execute thumb *glissandi* alone convincingly, then
the fifth finger feels more supported in passages such as this one from the
Brahms:

17 Leaps

> **'When real pianistic 'connection' occurs, it appears as though the performer is hardly moving at all.'**

One of the most important things to remember when playing the piano is the necessity of following the musical line in a passage where technical pyrotechnics can all too easily be perceived as the be all and end all. Liszt's 'La Campanella', arguably the most infamously challenging étude for leaps, suffers when performers fail to follow the melodic thread which is so clearly present in the right-hand thumb-notes throughout its duration:

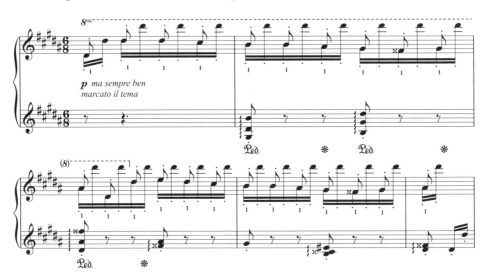

Tonal differentiation

Focusing on the shaping, direction and quality of sound in these pitches, by literally grasping onto them as a matter of musical necessity, the performer is given a lifeline which makes the challenges of the piece far less insurmountable. The most vital melodic line of the étude is then given a deeper tonal perspective, whilst the higher pitches (executed mainly by the fifth finger) are immediately given a more *leggiero* touch. The tonal differentiation between contrasted musical elements in passages where the performer has to jump around the keyboard like a demented kangaroo is absolutely vital. This can be clearly seen in another of Liszt's 'war-horse' études, 'Mazeppa', from the Transcendental set. As in 'La Campanella', it is important for the performer to emphasize the depth of tone in the main melodic component. In the case of 'Mazeppa' this involves chordal writing where the use of arm weight should be offset by the lighter, more finger-based approach necessary for the fast semiquaver and quaver runs that occur within the melody in its various presentations:

Trigger movement exercises

But what of the mechanical nitty-gritty involved? Above all, stiffness of the joints should be avoided at all costs. There are useful trigger movement exercises which should be practised. Try leaping with the left-hand thumb from one C to another two octaves higher as quickly as possible, but try to feel that the execution of the lower C is the beginning of the leap to the upper C:

Feel the two-octave leap as a single movement.

This 'play-leap' approach is essential for success in the octave jumps towards the end of the final movement of Brahms' Piano Concerto in D minor:

It is surprising to observe the number of students who view this type of problem as a threefold process – play low note(s), jump, then play upper note(s) – rather than as a two-movement one.

Silent jump exercises

There are wonderful 'silent jump' exercises too: try isolating the two notes which prove challenging. Play the first note then jump and rest on the second note, but refrain from playing it out loud. Then try with your eyes shut. This can prove very beneficial, as can the reverse: start by silently resting your finger on the lower note of the leap, then swiftly jump onto the higher note and play it as written.

Staple shape

Another worthwhile exercise is always to make sure that you arrive on the second note of a leap in advance of its execution. In quick-fire movements, such as from bar 213 of the left hand of Schumann's Toccata in C major, it may help literally to draw a staple shape from one octave to the next: play the octave, lift it up straight, move horizontally until your fingers are directly over the lower octave, then descend in a straight line:

Curve shape

Space forbids more than a short mention of passages where you should try to draw a curve in the air:

(Opening of the final variation of Rachmaninov's 'Paganini Rhapsody'.)

Adding extra notes

There are other examples where it can help in practice to play a thumb note an octave below the fifth-finger notes in order to 'stabilise' the hand:

(Closing arpeggio flourishes in the Scherzo section of Schubert's 'Wanderer Fantasy', firstly as in the original, secondly with addded thumb notes.)

Lateral thinking

Technical difficulties are often caused in jumps by the way the movement is perceived. If one thinks only in terms of upward ascent in a pattern of right-hand tenths at the piano, such as C-E2-E1-G2-G1-C3-C2 etc., then clearly a tiring time lies ahead:

However, if the view is taken that the first note is an 'extra', and that thereafter the passage in question is nothing more complex than a series of descending octaves, then technical lucidity and confidence will quickly emerge.

Horizontal thrusts

This is not to give *carte blanche* to 'arrangements' between the hands, for more often than not simplification via help from the other hand results in musical emasculation of the passage in question. For this reason, I would never advise performing the opening octave leap of Beethoven's Sonata Op.111 with two hands: the passage really needs the dramatic sweep obtained by one rapid horizontal thrust from the left hand alone.

'Horizontal thrusts' (if considered as single physical movements) can often provide solutions to technical problems. Quite often difficulties arise because leaps are perceived in terms of many small vertical movements rather than one larger, horizontal gesture. Debussy's 'Pour Les Octaves' étude is a case in point, where concentration on the melodic line, the horizontal flow of the right hand and the sense of organic connection to the keyboard can make the difference between a detached, splashy rendering and a really vital, warm-blooded and sparkling realisation. Clipped, percussive sounds are so much harder to leap from, whereas rounded, sonorous playing encourages relaxed, confident travel from note to note. Indeed, when real pianistic connection occurs, it appears as though the performer is hardly moving at all.

18 The sustaining pedal

'Poor pedalling usually results in a lack of clarity in the texture and confusion for the listener…'

The sustaining pedal may or may not be the soul of the piano, as Anton Rubinstein reportedly once claimed it to be[45], but there is little doubt that sensitive and intelligent use of it can transform your playing for the better. Many performances, particularly at an amateur level, suffer from a lack of awareness of the consequences of a cavalier pedal technique. As is often the case with piano playing, being able to listen effectively as you practise is essential. This, along with the cultivation of specific pedalling skills, will greatly improve your ability to use it with conviction. Sensitivity to the style and genre should also be considered, but as you become accustomed to the kind of pedalling that is appropriate for a given work, you can become more creative and spontaneous when particular pianos, acoustics and inspired moments bring forth unorthodox solutions.

Practice and development

Skilful pedalling greatly enhances the quality of playing, adding tonal richness and an infinite variety of possibilities for characterisation and technical enhancement. Poor pedalling usually results in a lack of clarity in the texture and confusion for the listener. So clearly it is important to know how to practise and develop your foot work. Let's begin with a run-down of technical set-up requirements for control in this crucial area of pianism.

Dig your right heel into the carpet and angle your foot to about 30°. The splay-foot position is most effective and comfortable not only for pedalling but also for resting your feet on the floor in non-pedalled passages. During operation it is important that only a small part of your right foot remains in contact with the sustaining pedal, and that only the smallest area of the pedal itself is depressed. Do not under any circumstances depress the pedal with more of your foot than you need to. Less is more when it comes to controlling sounds.

Individual preference will determine exactly which part of your body makes contact with the pedal. (Pianists tend to choose either part of the big toe, the ball or joint directly below the big toe, or as small an alternative area of the foot as possible.) Check your technique by taking your shoes off and observing the exact point where your foot makes contact with the pedal. In my case direct contact with the pedal is consistently made by the big joint below my big toe. This means that my sesamoid bones always depress the pedal. I am very consistent in choosing which part of the pedal to depress: my sesamoid bones make contact with the extreme right side lower corner of the pedal only. As

45 http://en.wikipedia.org/wiki/Anton_Rubinstein

already mentioned, my feet always adopt a balletic or Charlie Chaplin-like angle.

During pedalling it will feel comfortable if you use your heel as a pivot point and feel as light and relaxed as possible in the rest of your foot. Failure to do this can lead to stiffness and aches, so do be careful. Stiffness or lack of coordination from the ball of your foot can lead to sesamoiditis below your big toe, which is not pleasant. Practise lifting and dropping your foot onto the pedal (whilst keeping your heel firmly anchored on the carpet) until co-ordination and ease of movement becomes second nature. Though it can on occasion be dramatically exciting to lunge suddenly downwards with your foot for a *sforzando* attack, in general the principle of 'touch and press' which was emphasised for finger technique earlier should be reflected in your pedalling. Make sure that your foot is resting on the pedal before it depresses the mechanism. Try to avoid making 'pedal noise' as you work with your feet. Indeed it is important to avoid extraneous foot tapping sounds unless you feel specifically motivated to include them as an enhancing interpretive agent (for example in particular popular works that require stomping effects).

Preliminary exercise for *legato* pedalling

It is usually the norm to change pedal immediately after, rather than before (or simultaneously with) a change of chord. Here is a useful coordination exercise that will help you play with *legato* pedalling (slight overlaps of pedal between notes) and so aid facility and control.

Practise *legato* (or 'syncopated') pedalling by playing a C major scale through one octave, using only one finger but ensuring that there is no gap between notes. Depress the pedal and play middle C. Then play D, but as soon as the note sounds, release and re-take the pedal. There will be a split second in which the C and D are joined together by pedal. Next play E, and as soon as the note sounds again release and re-take the pedal, continuing in the same fashion through the scale. Let's extend this exercise by going to the opening of the slow movement of Beethoven's 'Pathetique' Sonata, Op.13:

The top-line melody notes need to overlap seamlessly in this excerpt. Although the fingers can connect most of these, it is simply not possible to achieve a perfect *legato* here unless your right foot is able to overlap and bind pairs of notes together. Adopt the same approach as in the *legato* scale exercise and the *cantabile* Beethoven clearly intended here will be possible.

How far you actually depress the pedal is an interesting point, and will largely depend on the quality of the instrument you possess. Of course in upright pianos the mechanism is limited, but experimentation is required to ascertain the exact point at which the pedal actually sustains sounds. On grand pianos and with lots of practice it is possible to find four (possibly five) levels of depression which will allow you to bind sounds together in a variety of contrasting ways. These range from the smallest level of depression for so called 'invisible' pedalling (similar to small finger overlaps between notes) to full depression down to the floor (useful when dealing with the thickest chords in Rachmaninov concertos). Every instrument varies in respect to pedal action, and it is always fascinating to note how they differ. There is no reason for elementary players to be excluded from refined pedalling as every pianist is potentially capable of distinguishing clearly between three or four levels of 'pedal descent' ('pedal depression' sounds too negative!).

A word of caution

When practising pedalling, always bear in mind that 'less is more'. The reality is that most musical contexts do not require full descent of the sustaining pedal. Much more clarity and control will arise if you only partially depress the mechanism. As mentioned, every instrument varies in terms of pedal resistance. Taking time to acclimatise to the pedal mechanism on an unfamiliar instrument can be even more of an issue for professional pianists than adjusting to the action of the keyboard. It is important therefore that you regularly experiment at your piano to discover how little (or indeed how much) you need to move the pedal down until it makes any impact. You will immediately find a range of new possibilities and variations.

Never fall into the habit of hiding sins of the fingers through over-generous use of the sustaining pedal. Clarity and lucidity should always be ideals in performance, and sensible pedalling can help to focus technical intentions by emphasising 'pivot' notes that can lead to complete security. Similarly, pedalling can be used as a distracting agent, whereby the performer focuses on one musical strand, so forgetting angst over another, which miraculously becomes completely accurate as a result. Wonderful examples of this phenomenon can be found in many a Liszt étude (such as 'La Campanella' and 'Mazeppa') in which pedalling to enhance melodic continuity can focus the player's attention on the 'easy' (but absolutely crucial) strand, thus liberating the mind from stress and resulting in accuracy by default.

Chopin's Étude in C sharp minor Op.25 No.7 is a good example of a somewhat slower pace of pedalling emphasising the melodic flow of the work. The pedal markings below help to sustain the long melody notes:

Finger pedalling

Always return periodically to your music by playing even very familiar
repertoire through without any pedal use at all. This will help you to hear
precisely where you need to move your right foot, and to use the pedal at those
points as a gluing agent. Do remember that overlapping with your fingers
alone (so called 'finger pedalling') can often be more than sufficient. Moreover,
when it comes to public venues, resonant acoustics in themselves often make
unpedalled performances sound sonically enhanced (or even overly resonant)
so one should be aware of the fact that what works in a small practice studio
with your feet could prove to be totally ineffective in a hall.

The amount and the way in which we choose to pedal depends on the stylistic
context as well as on our own interpretation. In 18th-century repertoire it
can be exhilarating to abandon all pedalling and rely on finger overlaps as a
secure substitute instead. Who could deny that it is miraculous to hear András
Schiff perform Bach's entire 'Well-Tempered Clavier' Book 1 with no use of the
sustaining pedal?[46] Of course, to accomplish a feat as extraordinarily virtuosic
as this means developing an infinitely skilful and subtle finger technique. On a
much more down-to-earth level, being able to connect as many of the notes in
your repertoire with your fingers alone will certainly make you feel technically
secure. And you may well need to have finger pedalling at the ready, too, if
your pedals cease to function altogether during a live concert. This famously
happened to the late John Ogdon during a live BBC Radio 3 broadcast of the
Chopin Op.10 études[47], which he was therefore forced to execute without any
right-foot support whatsoever. He was triumphantly able to continue playing
despite the fact that the sustaining pedal stopped working only a few minutes
into his performance!

Stylistically, you should be able to adjust your pedalling to fit in with the huge
range of sounds that the keyboard literature demands of its interpreters. This
takes you from quasi-invisible pedal dabs (such as those that are necessary
for repeated notes in Baroque fugal subjects) through to the Russian Romantic
repertoire where much longer overlapping between 'alien' harmonies can be
extremely expressive. In Rachmaninov, Medtner and Scriabin in particular
it is idiomatic to allow your pedalling to become at least a little bit 'dirty'.
Enjoy holding down the sustaining pedal through different chords. If you can
manipulate and balance your textures in such a way that the bass notes are not

---

46   Schiff achieved this extraordinary feat in a live performance from memory of all 24 Preludes and
Fugues at the Royal Northern College of Music on 19 November 2013.
47   BBC live broadcast from the 1960s.

too heavy and prominent, then 'dirty' Romantic footwork will most certainly be preferable to clipped pedalling that makes the textures overly clean and clinical. Many people associate this approach with pianists from Russia. A good example of 'Russian' pedalling can be seen in Rachmaninov's Prelude in D major Op.23 No.4, where the chord changes can be delayed considerably. This seems the musical equivalent of a watercolour artist's approach, washing one strand of paint into another:

In conclusion

As we have seen, pedal technique varies not only between different periods and composers, but also according to your own interpretative ideas for particular contexts and styles[48]. At the highest level there can be a tremendous synthesis between phrasing, *rubato*, pedalling and dynamic shading, all unifying an interpretation by emphasising 'the grand line' that runs through all masterpieces in the repertoire from pre-Bach to post-Bartók. Many of the great Chopin performances from Arthur Rubinstein, for example, stand as illustrations of this, so simple and beautiful is the artistry, with every technical aspect of the playing working in perfect synthesis. Let's close by remembering that pedalling is similar to all aspects of piano technique in that its success or failure ultimately depends on sensitive listening. Experience and perseverance will lead to success. Use your ears, your listeners' ears and recording devices for feedback. Intermediate players upwards may find it inspiring to refine their pedal skills through regular experimentation with Chopin's famous Prelude in E minor Op.28 No.4 (bars 1–3 below). Small pedal depression is all that is needed here, and the aim is to achieve a seamless *legatissimo*. Clearly the pedal needs to change with the changes of harmony, and the challenge is to manage your footwork in such a way to avoid accentuation and/or smudges to the texture:

---

48 For more detailed analysis of the use of all three pedals see Joseph Banowetz: 'The Pianist's Guide to Pedalling', Indiana University Press (1992).

19 The *una corda*

'… a vital tool for voicing chord progressions, separating a melodic line from accompaniment notes and altering tonal colours in a piece of music.'

Also known as the *sordino*, left, muting and soft pedal, *una corda* in piano music is a direction to play with this pedal depressed. An alternative name, for modern grand pianos at least, might be the shifting pedal, as it literally moves all of the hammers slightly to the right, '…so that the hammers strike only two of the three strings provided for each note in the treble and only one of the two strings provided for each note in the bass, while continuing to strike the single strings of the extreme bass…' (The New Grove Dictionary of Music and Musicians, Second Edition[49]).

Depressing the *una corda* pedal on a modern grand piano has the effect of both reducing the volume and changing the timbre of a note, making it softer and less brilliant. As such the pedal is more a colouring than a muting device, and by depressing it to varying degrees a range of sounds can be achieved. In this respect it is similar to the right, sustaining pedal – it has several levels of effect. Where the two pedals differ is in the variety of sounds that can result from one piano to the next, which is more considerable with the *una corda* than with sustaining pedal. On an upright piano the left-pedal action is less complicated – the pedal simply moves the hammers closer to the strings, thereby shortening their stroke and reducing the volume of the note, but not its timbre. Unfortunately pianists who do not play on a grand piano cannot really experience true *una corda* playing. Indeed, the left pedal presents one of the main differences between upright and grand instruments.

The function of the *una corda* pedal

The *una corda* has several functions depending on style and context. It is a vital tool for voicing chord progressions, separating a melodic line from accompaniment notes, and altering tonal colours in a piece of music. Depressing the pedal very slightly can also take the metallic edge off an inferior instrument. Historically, the *una corda* pedal became a feature of most grand pianos from the latter part of the 18th century. According to The New Grove Dictionary of Music and Musicians[50]: 'In pianos of the 18th and early 19th centuries, the *una corda* pedal caused the action to be shifted so far that the hammers struck only one string throughout the entire range of the instrument, giving the pianist a choice between *tre corde* (when the pedal was not

49 The New Grove Dictionary of Music and Musicians, 2nd edition (2001)
50 Ibid

depressed), *due corde* (partly depressed) and *una corda* (depressed completely).'
The use of this pedal on a modern grand piano when playing music written
before the latter half of the 19th century, or indeed when playing music
written before the *una corda* pedal was invented, is therefore often a cause of
controversy. Nonetheless, the request by the composer for its use should, in
most cases, be met by performers on modern instruments today, because they
will need in these contexts to express a hushed change of colour, even if they
can never hope to reproduce exactly what the composer intended.

Use of *una corda*

Much more controversial is the use of the *una corda* when it is not requested
by composers, particularly pre-19th century. In the harpsichord repertoire it
is possible to interpret changes of registration via *una corda* use (i.e. in echo
passages), although anything that becomes predictable or overused in this
context will unquestionably annoy listeners. As with the sustaining pedal,
caution and taste remain the important considerations – the *una corda* pedal
should be used sparingly and with careful thought. Overuse can stifle music
below a *mezzo piano* dynamic level, and it is essential to maintain a relaxed and
controlled technique so as to avoid relying on the pedal as a 'security blanket'.
The *pianissimo* passage during the opening of Beethoven's 'Appassionata'
Piano Sonata in F minor Op.57 No.23, for example, is far more exciting without
the use of the *una corda* pedal, even if it is infinitely more challenging to play
without the aid of your left foot. It is also advisable to avoid suddenly using the
pedal in the middle of a phrase, as the change in colour can sound strange and
interrupt the musical flow.

Multi-levelled pedalling

The technique of multi-levelled pedalling mentioned in Chapter 18 for the
sustaining pedal can also be applied to the left pedal and should be considered
a standard technical procedure. (Of course this unfortunately will not work
on an upright instrument where the pedal mechanism allows for only one
change in sound, regardless of how shallow or deep your left-foot pedalling
is.) Dig your heel into the carpet and centre your weight on it, rather than on
your toes. As with your right foot, the point of pedal contact itself should be the
ball immediately below your big toe. When using the *una corda*, you can lightly
apply the ball below your big toe to the left-hand lower corner of the pedal. Do
not view contact with the *una corda* as a default position of rest. Experience
has shown that a feeling of solidity, firmness and contact with the floor which
comes directly from the heel rather than toes will lead to more clarity, control
and efficiency in pedalling technique. It is always fascinating to see just how
small the distance is that you need to depress the *una corda* for a significant
change in tone to be produced. Pianists of all levels can try this, and should find
experimentation immediately revelatory.

As with sustaining pedals, *una cordas* vary enormously in sound quality and resistance from instrument to instrument. If you have an unsympathetic piano with an abrasive sound or even just a slightly metallic tone, depressing the *una corda* by the smallest of margins can make an enormous difference. Its judicious use can indeed instantly transform percussively aggressive playing into relatively warm, sensitive music making. Chopin's 'Berceuse' is a miniature miracle in terms of variety of colour, and the performer has many choices with regards to the use of the *una corda*:

Degrees of pedalling

Whilst many would consider it too simplistic a solution simply to depress the pedal at the beginning of this piece and keep it depressed until after the final bar, it is almost as crude to think only in terms of using it (or not using it) for particular phrases. Bearing in mind individual pianos and acoustics will inevitably affect pedalling, at bar 34 I would apply a deep use of the *una corda*, while bars 35–36, with their sparkling *mezzo staccato* right-hand triads, work best with shallow pedal. At bar 37 the subtle shift in colour can be emphasised by a medium approach to the pedal. Of course, by applying three different levels of the *una corda* within the four-bar segment there will inevitably be a change in approach technically. The pedalling will reinforce and stimulate variety of colour, not only by what it does but by what it implies. In this context, bar 34 could be played with deep key-bedding, plenty of overlapping *legato* and a close hand. By contrast, bar 35 could be played with the right hand lifting the triads off the keyboard, and at bar 37 you could adopt an approach in which the 'spider-web' right-hand figurations are played tepidly, with some overlapping, but with the finger work executed nearer the surface of the keys than in bar 34.

In a concerto context it is dangerous to use the *una corda* when the projection of a melody is vital. The two simple solo entries in the slow movement of Grieg's Piano Concerto provide a case in point. This is 'open air' music, evocative of mountain scenery and outdoor spaciousness. The piano should fill the hall with power within the hushed dynamic range. In order to sculpt a sonority that will capture the audience even at the back of London's Royal Festival Hall, a less conventional approach to the *una corda* must be adopted. However, there may well be a case for using this pedal in concerto passages where accompaniment figurations need to be off-set against melodic lines. In the excerpt below from the Grieg Concerto an argument could be made for covering the left-hand notes 4-7 of each bar with *una corda*. But such usage requires careful handling, with quick release so that the right-hand line remains totally unaffected.

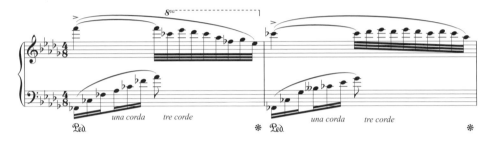

Sometimes we simply need to celebrate and indulge by using *una corda* to the full. This is certainly the case from the opening onwards of the rare, exquisite miniature 'In the Glen' by the Scottish Romantic, Hamish MacCunn (1868-1916). As this is unquestionably an example of golden-age pianistic glory, it simply cries out for constant *una corda* usage in the manner of Paderewski (who reputedly used the *una corda* in every dynamic context, even loud passages). Prepare the opening of 'In the Glen' by 'laying the carpet' (depressing both pedals in advance). You can then enjoy the deliciously veiled, sonorous sweetness that results, especially when the music rises to *forte*. Modern pedagogues may well have apoplexy at this suggestion, but the resultant sounds will have an appropriately cultivated aura, one that will immediately transport listeners back to the era in which the piece was written:

Hamish MacCunn 'In the Glen'

20 The *sostenuto* or middle pedal

> '...the clarity and precision of the middle pedal means that great focus and definition in the textures makes the music more defined and vivid in terms of colour and articulation.'

Though there were isolated examples prior to 1874 of instruments equipped with pedal mechanisms that enabled pianists to hold specific notes without affecting other notes, it is generally acknowledged that Albert Steinway 'invented' the middle pedal when he patented it in that year.[51] Over the years it has had a variety of names (Steinway, *sostenuto* and organ pedal to name but a few) and generally a mysterious image, even amongst professional performers.

Sadly, ignorance has remained the rule as far as its use is concerned in many circles, and it is alarming to note how few students today realise that three conditions need to be remembered for the pedal to function effectively:

1 It will *only* work if you catch the notes you wish it to hold by playing them with your fingers (either out loud or silently) before you depress it with your foot (normally but by no means always your left foot).

2 It will *not* work if you depress it simultaneously with the sustaining (right) pedal or try to depress it whilst the sustaining pedal is depressed.

3 It will *not* work if you lift it up even slightly whilst using it. This causes extra and unwanted notes to be caught in the held sonority, leading to untidiness and hazy textures.

Achieving greater clarity

Repertoire written in the golden age of piano playing is the most natural for the middle pedal, especially transcriptions of organ works by Busoni and others. It is easy to see the benefits of this pedal in the extended pedal points of, for example, Tausig's or Busoni's transcriptions of the Bach D minor Organ Toccata, or in Busoni's celebrated transcription of the Bach Violin Chaconne. Moreover this music seems to benefit from the use of the middle pedal as a means towards greater clarity than would be possible from the sustaining pedal:

51 Joseph Banowetz Ibid

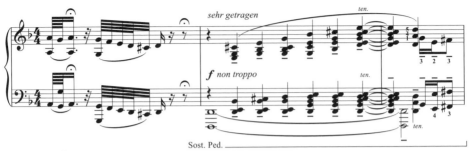

Bach D minor Organ Toccata

By depressing and holding an octave continuously for passages of 20 or 30 bars, a tremendous build-up of sonority can result, as the held octave inevitably gets louder and louder with each repetition. This can sound like a massive orchestral *crescendo*; the clarity and precision of the middle pedal means that great focus and definition in the textures makes the music more defined and vivid in terms of colour and articulation:

Ostinato

The middle pedal can be used effectively for *ostinato* figures higher up the keyboard too. In the continuous middle-register three-note ostinato (D-C♯-C♮) from Prokofiev's 'Désespoir' Op.4 No.3 it is possible to create a hypnotically charged bell effect by silently depressing the D and catching it with the middle pedal prior to playing the first note of the piece out loud.[52] Hold down without letting go for the first 36 bars. Such silent manoeuvres can be extremely effective in using this pedal, provided that the resulting sonorities enhance rather than detract from the character of the passage in question. In the Prokofiev you will need to use all three pedals at the same time: the subdued

---

52　I did this in my own recording of this piece on the Olympia label back in 1989 on 'Prokofiev Piano Sonatas Volume 1' OCD 255.

atmosphere means that the *una corda* must be utilised. Swivel from the ball of your big toe round to the left so that your heel can depress the left pedal. This takes lots of patience and practice, but it is worth persevering. Once the left hand enters the piece you will find that the sustaining pedal also needs to be used. But because you are already holding down the middle pedal constantly, it is possible to be refined, subtle and sparing with its use.

Contrapuntal textures

The middle pedal can be used to clarify contrapuntal textures by sustaining *legato* lines and chords and thus liberating other strands in textures for drier execution. In such circumstances it can appear as though more than one pianist is playing. Percy Grainger's rich and memorable collection of piano works comes immediately to mind here. Indeed, his specific indications for the use of the middle pedal surely remain the most detailed and painstakingly precise of any composer of piano music. As a great testament to the use of the middle pedal, one can do no better than cite Grainger's performing edition of the Grieg Piano Concerto (Schirmer) written with the full endorsement of Grieg himself[53]. It is extraordinary to study all the instructions in this publication, full of wonderful insights into colour, phrasing and technical control. Even if it is not realistic for a performer today to follow every middle-pedal 'Graingerism' in this edition, by studying the instructions carefully it is possible to master the middle pedal art in most contexts.

Smaller hands and awkward stretches

On a purely practical level the middle pedal can be useful for players with small hands. Those who find it hard to stretch more than an octave yet wish to play repertoire requiring large chords will find that this pedal sustains sonority without the ugliness that can sometimes result from the use of the sustaining pedal. Many an upward stretch in Beethoven, for example, can be clarified if the lowest note in the chord is caught quickly in the middle pedal and followed by arpeggiation:

(catch B♭ in middle pedal)   *Beethoven Sonata in E♭ Op.81a (2nd movement)*

In this example, those who are unable to stretch a tenth have time quickly to catch the left-hand low B flat with the middle pedal before the beginning of bar 20 and so sustain this sound through the two bars that require it, achieving a clarity and control of sound that would not be otherwise possible.

53 Grieg Piano Concerto in A minor, edited Grainger Ibid.

Similarly, linear clarity and shaping can be enhanced if awkward stretches in a melody line are neutralised by capturing isolated notes in this pedal and holding them on for longer than their written value. It goes without saying that lots of practice and experimentation is necessary here, and it is vital that the end result hides the use of the pedal to the listener as much as possible.

Appendix 1

Basic exercises for daily warm-up sessions at the keyboard

1 Basic posture-check, with weight balanced between the feet, standing up first, then with same approach seated. Check stool is at the correct height and distance from the keys. Straight back and relaxed neck.

- Dropping and flopping.
- **Imaginary suspension of both arms from strings** with complete relaxation.
- **Feeling blood circulation to the finger-tips.**

2 'Gripping' exercises with firm fingers but relaxation behind them; put fingers down on 8 notes then check thumbs, wrists, elbows, shoulders, neck and trunk in turn.

repeat many
times with varied
dynamics

3 Basic five-finger independence exercise with all five fingers on the keys and each one playing in turn. No other movement is allowed. To be played with complete relaxation and good posture. Play non *legato*, *staccato* and *legato* in turn.

4 Trill exercise in triplets: *legato* only and in each hand. This uses the same principles as (3) above.

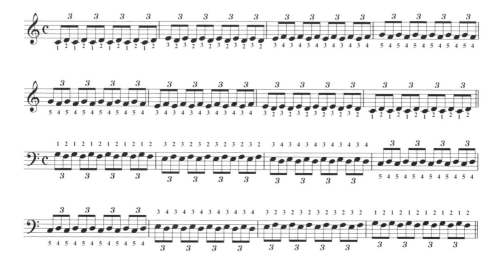

5 Basic thumbing-under exercises using major and minor triads on white notes, firstly with fingering 1-3-1-3-1 then 1-2-3-1-3-2-1 in both hands (contrary motion principle as shown below).

6 Arm-weight exercise using three-note then four-note chords.

etc

etc

7 'Supermarket trolley' exercise in single notes (the arm moves the hand rather than the hand moving the arm). This is then extended to become octaves.

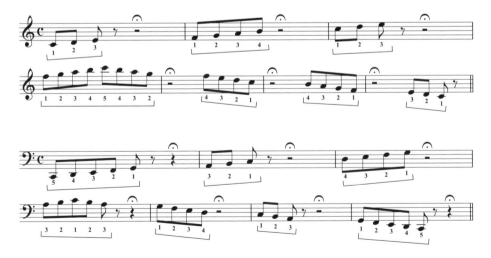

8 Single-note scales using fifth finger alone and each hand separately, trying to join the notes in sonority and thus striving for deep tone and relaxation of the wrists. Firstly in the right hand with a one-octave C major scale descending (slowly, using the fifth then the first fingers). Then in the left hand with an ascending one-octave C major scale using the same fingers in turn.

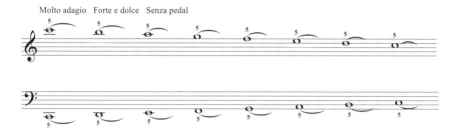

Appendix 2

Examples of polyrhythm scales

Appendix 3

Reflex exercises

Thumb velocity and suppleness needs to be developed and built up to virtuoso level. Single-note thumb scales and arpeggios should be practised with the metronome to at least crotchet = 120, with four notes per beat. This is good preparation for octave work and should be done with loose wrists, close contact to the keyboard and no stiffness in the arms, shoulders, neck or back. Rapid arpeggio work in all keys for the thumb alone is also to be recommended for development over a long period. Providing it is done with the feeling that the thumb is sliding over the keys rather than hopping, this will reinforce a well-coordinated approach to secure position shifts and eventually effortless accuracy not only in rapid octave work, but also in passages demanding fast chordal shifts.

The exercises below should be practised as a natural extension of the basic *staccato* exercises outlined in Chapter 6. They all need to be worked at with freedom of movement. Avoid becoming overly heavy in practice; aim for short sessions of work and try to keep the dynamic level down as a quieter range of sounds will focus your concentration more effectively. Above all, listen to your body. Do not do anything that feels uncomfortable or even awkward. It is important that you avoid locking your wrists, elbows, shoulders and neck. Try to play on the surface of the keys, aiming for a *leggiero* touch, and to make each exercise sound like a *glissando*. Try them all hands separately as well as together (if appropriate). For variety, transpose all the exercises into different major and minor keys. You should also try them out at different octaves.

The first two exercises are excellent preparatory studies for octave playing. Exercise 1 should be thought of as a study in 'thrusting movement'. As you play groups of 2 then 3, 4, and 5 notes (and so on), feel that you are making just one big arm movement per beat. Confidence and freedom are the keys to success here, so do begin each beat from as high above the keyboard as possible! Work at this study with both hands separately, then together (left hand an octave lower than written). Once you have mastered it with fifth fingers alone, try it with each of the other fingers in turn.

Exercise 1

Exercise 2 for the fifth finger alone requires freedom from the wrist and the ability to prepare each note in advance by getting over it a split second before you actually depress it. It is useful to try this exercise with your eyes shut and also with the fourth, third, second and first fingers alone. Work at it hands separately then together before tackling it in other keys. It is extremely good for improving a sense of pianistic geography, giving players more confidence in their ability to move rapidly around the keyboard.

Exercise 2

Exercise 3 extends the scratching finger-*staccato* technique as outlined in Chapter 6. Strive to make it sound like a series of *glissandos* and play with minimum movement in the hands, wrists and arms. It should be transposed into all keys and practised both separately and hands together.

Exercise 3

Exercise 4 speaks for itself and is a test of stamina. Once you can play the scale pattern with the fifth finger, try it with each of the others in turn too. It can be stimulating to use the metronome as a means of building up velocity here, but do be careful: in exercises of this nature, injury through strain can occur all too easily.

Exercise 4

Exercises 5a, b and c are repeated-note challenges without finger changes. Working with coordination in this way can loosen your wrists and give you more pliability. Many people mistakenly believe that you need to change fingers in order to play repeated notes effectively. Working on these exercises will demonstrate that it is possible to build up considerable control and flair using the same fingering throughout. Try 5a with each finger in turn, hands separately and together. In 5b and 6 you can drop down for each 'thrust' of repeated notes from as high a position above the keyboard as you wish (in this respect they are similar to exercise 1).

Exercise 5

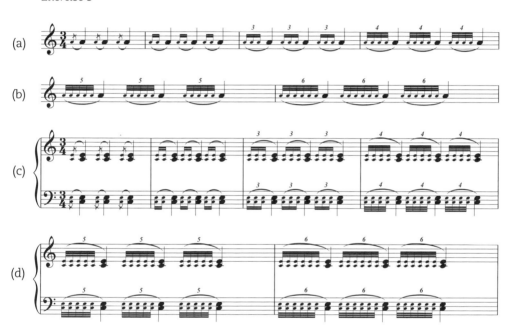

Exercise 6

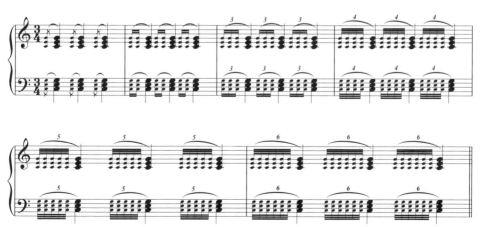

Finally, exercises 7a–d show the influence of drumming. In the early stages of
building up stick technique, percussion players hone their control by endlessly
working with left-hand / right-hand hits in alternation (so-called 'Mummy,
Daddy, Mummy, Daddy' work). Pianists need to develop similar skills if they are
to be able to cope with music that demands such hand movement in rapid-fire
articulation (as in Gershwin's 'Rhapsody in Blue', Prokofiev's 'Toccata' and many
other pieces). Begin by tapping all four of them on the closed lid of the piano.
When this feels comfortable, start practising each exercise quietly, slowly and
lightly. Feel a springy pliability in the wrist: the aim should be for each sound to
bounce into the next. Avoid stiffness and tension at all costs.

Exercise 7

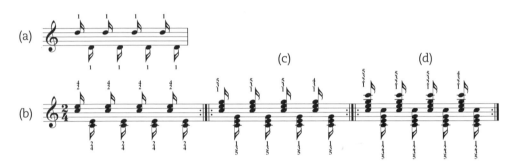